GEORGE NATHAN1

THE PAMIRS

AND

THE SOURCE OF THE OXUS

Elibron Classics
www.elibron.com

THE PAMIRS

AND

THE SOURCE OF THE OXUS.

BY THE

RIGHT HON. GEORGE N. CURZON, M.P.,

GOLD MEDALLIST OF THE ROYAL GEOGRAPHICAL SOCIETY.

WITH MAP AND ILLUSTRATIONS.

Revised, and reprinted from 'The Geographical Journal' for July, August, and September, 1896.

LONDON:

THE ROYAL GEOGRAPHICAL SOCIETY, 1, SAVILE ROW;

EDWARD STANFORD, 26 AND 27, COCKSPUR STREET, CHARING CROSS, S.W.

THE PAMIRS AND THE SOURCE OF THE OXUS.

THERE is a passage in a now too-little-read book by a famous author that depicts the very curiosity whereby I was led in the autumn of 1894 to make the geographical researches which this essay will attempt to record. In his 'Anatomy of Melancholy,' the ingenious Burton, summarizing the problems of natural history or physical geography which he would fain have solved, speaks thus: " I would examine the Caspian Sea, and see where and how it exonerates itself after it hath taken in Volga, Iaxares, Oxus, and those great rivers. I would find out with Trajan the fountains of Danubius, of Ganges, and of Oxus." To myself also the Oxus, that great parent stream of humanity, which has equally impressed the imagination of Greek and Arab, of Chinese and Tartar, and which, from a period over three thousand years ago, has successively figured in the literature of the Sanskrit Puranas, the Alexandrian historians, and the Arab geographers, had always similarly appealed. Descending from the hidden "Roof of the World," its waters tell of forgotten peoples, and whisper secrets of unknown lands. They are believed to have rocked the cradle of our race. Long the legendary water-mark between Iran and Turan, they have furrowed a deep channel in the destinies and character of mankind. Already in 1888 I had crossed the Oxus in its middle course at Charjui, in the now Russianized territories of Bokhara. There, in the beautiful words of our English poet, I had beheld how—

> " The majestic river floated on
> Out of the mist and hum of that low lan l,
> Into the frosty starlight, and there moved
> Rejoicing through the hushed Chorasmian waste
> Under the solitary moon."

But the Oxus then before me was the Oxus of the plains only; it was—

> " Oxus forgetting the bright speed he had
> In his high mountain-cradle of Pamere."

And, with the poet, my imagination had flown eastwards and upwards to that aërial source, and had longed to pierce the secrets that were

A

hidden behind the glaciers of the Pamirs and the snowy sentinels of the Hindu Kush. Where did this great river really rise? Which among the several confluents of its upper course was the true parent stream? This was a question that had been obscured by the imperfect information or the erroneous hypotheses of previous travellers, as well as complicated by the diplomatic sophistries of rival statesmen. At least four separate and mutually destructive claims had been made to the honour of parentage. It was in the main, so far as geography is concerned, in order to solve these doubts, and at the same time to see from personal observation those much debated lands of the Pamir or Pamirs, which have been variously represented as grassy plains and horrible wildernesses, as a certain death-trap for invading armies, and yet as the vulnerable gates of Hindustan, that I planned the journey which I now proceed to sketch. In dealing with it, I shall pass lightly over all other portions but those relating to the Upper Oxus valley and the Pamirs, in connection with which it is my desire in this paper to supply, so far as possible, a monograph of existing, though for the most part unpublished, information about the regions within or contiguous to that area.

During the six months of my absence in the autumn and winter of 1894, I really undertook two distinct journeys, which had little but a common political interest to unite them. The first was to the Indian frontier states of the Hindu Kush, the Pamirs, and the Oxus. The second was to Afghanistan. The distance covered on horseback or on foot in the two was just short of 1800 miles, much of it over ground of great difficulty. The fact that, while on the Indian frontier and the Pamirs, I accomplished a daily average march of over 21 miles for fifty-four marching days, excluding halts, is no criterion of ordinary opportunities, since it was due solely to the exceptional kindness shown me by every British officer on the frontier, notably Captain Younghusband, a former Gold Medallist of this Society, as well as to the arrangements made in advance for my transport by the local chiefs and rajahs, notably by the Thum of Hunza, through whose territories I passed.

Similarly in Afghanistan, my daily marching average, with a large camp and an escort of over seventy men, was 27 miles. But this again was owing to the generous entertainment of the Amir, who laid out horses for me along the route. I make this explanation in order, on the one hand, to account for the apparent rapidity of a journey which, under ordinary conditions, would occupy probably nearly double the time, and, on the other hand, to disavow a credit to which I am not in the least entitled.

The first section of my journey was as follows. Leaving Srinagar, I marched up the military road that has been built since 1890 to connect the valley of Kashmir with the British military outpost of Gilgit.

This road is a little short of 200 miles in length, and crosses the Himalayas by one of two passes—the Burzil, which is 13,450 feet in height, and the Kamri, which is 300 feet lower. Of this part of the journey, however, since it is well described both in Mr. Knight's and Mr. Conway's books, I shall here say nothing. From Gilgit I followed the Hunza-Nagar valley to Baltit, the capital of Hunza; and from there, in the middle of September, my friend Mr. Lennard, a noted *shikari*, who in 1891 had shot *Ovis Poli* on the Taghdumbash Pamir, and I started forth, escorted by the Thum and his Wazir and a crowd of Hunza men, for the Kilik Pass, by which we passed from Anglo-Indian territory to the Chinese possession of the Taghdumbash Pamir. There we stayed a few days to shoot *Ovis Poli*, and then made our way across the eastern watershed of the Pamirs by the Wakh-jir Pass to the headwaters of the Oxus and the Pamir-i-Wakhan. From there I paid a visit to Lake Chakmak and the Little Pamir. For some mysterious reason, the Indian Government was averse to my going on to the Victoria Lake and the Great Pamir. Accordingly from here I retraced my steps, and Lennard and myself marched down the Oxus valley to Sarhad, the frontier outpost of Afghan arms in Wakhan. From there we recrossed the Hindu Kush by the low depression known as the Baroghil Pass, beyond which we separated—Lennard to return over the Darkot Pass, with its formidable snow and glaciers, to Yasin and Gilgit; I to follow down the gorge of the Yarkhun river (which in its later course is variously known as the Mastuj, Chitral, Kashkar, and Kunar river) to Mastuj. There I was joined by Captain Younghusband, Political Officer in Chitral, who accompanied me for a further distance of 65 miles down the same valley to the capital of that state, where we were hospitably entertained and treated with the greatest distinction by Nizam-ul-Mulk, the Mehtar or ruler, since treacherously murdered. From Chitral, finding it impossible to make, as I had hoped to do, the then untravelled but most important march to Peshawur, a distance only of 180 miles, or to Jellalabad, a distance of 160 miles, I was compelled to retrace my steps; and Captain Younghusband and I marched back to Mastuj, and from there, by the Chamarkand pass, Ghizar, Gupis, and Punial, along the valley of the Ghizar and Gilgit river, back to Gilgit. From Gilgit I followed down the Indus to the interesting post of Chilas, one of several small highland communities, of Aryan origin, inhabiting the mountainous and almost unexplored country called by themselves Shinkai. In 1892 Chilas passed into British hands, and is now the outpost of British arms among the frontier republics of the Indus valley. After leaving Chilas, I recrossed the Himalayas by the Babusar pass, 13,400 feet, and re-entered British Indian territory, descending to Abbottabad by the as yet little-known Khagan valley, which is the most direct route from Gilgit to any Indian military base. This was the termination of the first part of my journey.

When, a little later, I started for Afghanistan at the invitation of
the Amir, I marched up by the ordinary road from Peshawur through
the Khyber pass to Jellalabad and Kabul, a distance of 180 miles. This
time I was alone. After a fortnight in Kabul, the Amir gave me permission to leave his country by way of Kandahar; and accordingly I
marched down by the well-known route, 325 miles in length, passing
through Ghuzni and Kelat-i-Ghilzai to Kandahar, that was last traversed
by the armies of Sir Donald Stewart and Lord Roberts in 1880. From
Kandahar I rode 65 miles to Chaman, the British frontier outpost in
Beluchistan, where I again touched a railway and civilization. I shall
say nothing of my journey in Afghanistan here, since its main features
were of political rather than geographical interest; but shall revert at
once to my earlier experiences, both in approaching and, still more, after
crossing the Hindu Kush.

Upon the stupendous natural features of the region embraced by the
Himalayan and Hindu Kush ranges, comment has more than once been
made in papers read before this Society. Here a labyrinth of the highest
peaks in the world lift their unscaled pinnacles above the deepest
valleys, the most sombre ravines. Within a range of 70 miles, there are
eight crests with an elevation of over 24,000 feet, while the little state
of Hunza alone is said to contain more peaks of over 20,000 feet than
there are over 10,000 feet in the entire Alps. The longest glaciers in
the globe outside of the Arctic circle pour their frozen cataracts down the
riven and tortured hollows of the mountains. Great rivers foam and
thunder in flood-time along the resounding gorges, though sometimes
reduced in winter—the season of low waters—to errant threads.
Avalanches of snow, and—still more remarkable—of mud, come plung-
ing down the long slopes, and distort the face of nature as though by
some lamentable disease. In this great workshop of primæval forces,
wherever the imprisoned energies are not still at work, they have left
their indelible traces in the stormy outline of the crags, in the water-
marks of lakes that have burst their bounds and have fled, in the artificial structure of the alluvial terraces, in the deep scouring of the
impetuous streams.

There is, further, a certain gradation of landscape-impression, in the
northward march from Kashmir to the Pamirs, that is not without an
instructive as well as an æsthetic significance. On the earlier parts of
the road to Gilgit, the traveller rides through the shade of pine forests
and skirts romantic glens. Soon he passes into a region where there
are neither trees nor flowers, where the mountains exhibit only a sterile
and forbidding gradient, and where across the bald summits of the
passes the snow-laden gales shriek a sentence of death to animal and
man. The Indus valley, with its brown and verdureless rocks, enclosing
the Tartarean trough in which the inky volume of the great river rolls
by, accentuates the mournful impression. Then in the Hunza valley,

VALLEY AND RAKAPUSHI.

which is undoubtedly one of the most remarkable scenes in the world, Nature seems to exert her supremest energy, and in one chord to exhaust almost every note in her vast and majestic diapason of sound. She shows herself in the same moment tender and savage, radiant and appalling, the relentless spirit that hovers above the ice-towers, and the gentle patroness of the field and orchard, the tutelary deity of the haunts of men.

Never can I forget the abruptness and splendour of the surprise when, shortly after leaving the fort of Chalt, 30 miles beyond Gilgit, there burst upon our view the lordly apparition of the great mountain Rakapushi, lifting, above the boulder-strewn or forest-clad declivities of his lower stature, 18,000 feet of unsullied ice and snow to a total height of 25,550 feet above the sea. I shall always say that next to the sight of Kinchinjunga from beyond Darjiling, this is the finest mountain spectacle that I have seen. Rakapushi is one of the most superbly modelled of mountains. Everywhere visible, as we ascend the valley, he keeps watch and ward over the lower summits, and over the smiling belts of green and orchard-plots below that owe their existence to his glacial bounty. But up above his true and imperial majesty is best revealed. There enormous and shining glaciers fill the hollows of his sides, and only upon the needle point of his highest crest is the snow unable to settle. As we gaze at Rakapushi, indeed, we find an unconscious answer to the poet's query—

" What pleasure lives in height (the shepherd sang)—
In height and cold, the splendour of the hills ? "

For there, in more than fancy, we can—

" Walk
"With Death and Morning on the silver horns ; "

There before us are—

"The firths of ice
That huddling slant in furrow-cloven falls
To roll the torrent out of dusky doors."

And though our eye, aching with the dazzling vision, may seek a transient solace in the restful verdure of the lower and terraced slopes, and may even dip into the deep gorge where the river hums 1000 feet below our feet, yet it cannot for long resist the enchantment of those glimmering peaks, and ever hankers for the fascination of the summit.

The distance from Gilgit to Hunza is 61 miles, which we covered easily in three days. In former times, and up till the brilliant little campaign in the winter of 1891, by which the British became the practical masters of the country, the road, if it could be so called without a grim jest, consisted in many parts of rocky and ladder-like tracks up the mountain-sides, and of narrow galleries, built out with timbers, round the edges of the cliffs. It has since been much improved by the sappers attached to the Gilgit garrison. Outside Baltit, the capital of Hunza, we were

met by the Thum, or Mir, or Rajah, as he is variously called, Mohammed
Nazim Khan, a young man of about twenty-eight years of age, whom
the Indian Government invested with the ruling title after his elder
brother, Safdar Ali Khan, a murderer and fratricide of more than ordinary
activity, had fled before the British advance in 1891. The Thum was
accompanied by his Wazir, Humaiun Beg, the representative of a family
in which that dignity has been hereditary for generations, and himself
the most agreeable and capable personality in the Hindu Kush states.
I visited the Thum in the so-called castle of Baltit, a most picturesque
edifice—the model of a feudal baron's stronghold—that rises to a considerable height above the flat-roofed cubes of the town. I was received
in a chamber opening on to the roof, where the Russian explorer, Captain
Grombchevski, had opened negotiations with Safdar Ali Khan in 1888.
To this apartment it was necessary to ascend by a rude ladder, conducting to a hatchway in the floor. This might be thought a primitive
mood of entrance; but then the castle of Baltit (so called because it was
originally built by Baltis, from Baltistan) is not precisely a Windsor.

At Baltit, as also at Gilgit and at Chitral, I witnessed the native
game of polo, which, after being introduced into India by its Mussulman
conquerors nine hundred years ago, and having been the favourite game
of the Mogul Emperors, found a refuge in these two out-of-the-way
corners of the Hindu Kush states on the one hand, and Manipur on the
other, until about thirty years ago it was brought back to its former
haunts by the British officer. The Nagar men are reputed to be the
best players in the Hindu Kush area; but the Kanjutis (the name by
which the Hunza people are described north of the Hindu Kush) are little
inferior. The game, as most people know, is played on a narrow strip
of ground, frequently destitute of grass, surrounded by a low wall of
stones upon which the spectators take their seats, and from which the
ball rebounds into play. The ground at Hunza is about 280 yards in
length by 30 in width; but that at Chitral is wider, and has a curious
bay or projection at one side. The goals are low white stones fixed in
the ground, and at Hunza were only about 7 feet apart. The local
band, consisting of a big drum, a couple of kettledrums, and two or
three clarionets with a note very much like a bagpipe, accompany the
performance, and when a goal is scored indulge in the most frantic din.
The players, who range in number from four to twelve or more a-side,
ride the native ponies, with the roughest of bits, on the highest of
saddles, and use a much shorter polo-stick than is common in England,
an almond-wood handle being rudely fitted into a heavy plane or willow-
wood head. The native ball is of wood and is also very heavy; but the
British officers, who habitually join the natives in the game, have among
other reforms introduced the lighter English ball of bamboo-root. At
Baltit they have also Anglicized the indigenous game by reducing the'
absurd and indefensible number of players, by persuading them to

abandon the rule under which a goal was not scored until one of the side that had struck the ball between the posts had dismounted and picked it up, with the result of a frightful and even dangerous scuffle, and by somewhat modifying the pretty fashion of striking off. Under the native rules the opener of the game or the winner of the last goal galloped at full speed from one corner of the ground, with the whole of the rest of the field behind him, and when he came to the centre threw the ball into the air and struck it with his polo stick, frequently—such was the skill of the best players—scoring a goal from the stroke. There is a well-known Nagar player at the present moment who may usually be counted on for a goal in this fashion. At Baltit he now only gallops down one quarter of the distance before striking off; and his adversaries, awaiting him in the centre, have a chance of saving the goal. There is one respect, however, in which it is found difficult to modify the native practice, and that is in respect of " off-side " and " crossing," about which no scruple is entertained whatsoever. With its clumsy implements and with its ill-groomed steeds the native game of polo nevertheless excels in picturesqueness any that I have else-where witnessed. The men ride like demons, and perform feats of horsemanship of which the English game is innocent. At Chitral the beaten side had to dance to the victors ; and it was the particular pleasure of the Mehtar (since unhappily murdered) to select as captain of the opposite team to himself, which was invariably beaten, an old gentleman who had previously made an unsuccessful attempt upon his life, and upon whom it amused him to wreak this playful revenge.

From Baltit Lennard and I commenced our march to the Pamirs. The distance to the Kilik Pass is about 81 miles, over one of the worst tracks in the world. At a little beyond Baltit the valley of the Hunza river, which from Chalt has pursued an easterly course, turns due north, and the river cuts a deep gash or furrows an uproarious channel along its bottom in its descent from the watershed of the Pamirs. The scenery also changes. In place of the richly cultivated terraces and the abounding orchards of both the Hunza and the Nagar slopes in the lower valley, we find only rare villages and still rarer cultivation, and are in a region of rocks and stones. Big glaciers propel their petrified cascades to the very edge of the river. In many places this required to be forded. Sometimes the road is only conducted round the edge of the precipices that overhang the torrent by artificial ladders and ledges, built out from the cliff with stones loosely laid upon sup-ports of brushwood and timber jammed into the interstices of the rock. This sounds very dreadful, but in practice is much less alarming, the galleries, though only lasting for a few days, being sufficiently strong at the beginning, and being slightly inclined inwards toward the cliff. In the course of a very few days I underwent the bodily labours of a Parliamentary session, and parted with the superfluous physical accretions of an entire London season. Over this vile stretch of country there are two tracks, the upper or summer track, which avoids the river-bed, then filled with a fierce and swirling torrent, and climbs to the summit of the cliffs, several thousand feet above the water; and the lower or

THUM AND WAZIR OF HUNZA.

winter track, which can only be pursued when, the melting of the snow by the hot summer suns being over, the current dwindles to a number of fordable channels, across and amid the boulder-piled fringes of which the traveller picks his way. The second track is not commonly available till the beginning of October; but a few cloudy days had sensibly lowered the river, and it was thought that, with the aid of the Thum's people, who accompanied us in large numbers, the route might be found practicable, except in a few places where, to avoid the still swollen stream, we should require to scale the heights. The whole of our baggage, tents, etc., had to be carried on the backs of men, the route being quite impracticable for baggage-animals. We had riding-horses ourselves, but there were many places where these had to be abandoned and swum across the river. I was very favourably impressed with the Hunza men, who were strong, cheerful, and willing, and struck me as both the most masculine and the most agreeable of the Aryan tribes of the Hindu Kush. Those persons who contended that we should do an injury to them, and heap up trouble for ourselves, by interfering with their liberty, which, as interpreted by their chiefs, was merely the liberty to harry and plunder and slay their less manly or warlike neighbours, are shown to have talked nonsense, as croakers usually do. The people themselves extracted very little from the raids, the proceeds of which were commonly pocketed by the chiefs; and I have no doubt that many a converted freebooter lent a not unwilling back to the transport of our loads.

Perhaps the least agreeable part of the journey was the compulsory fording of the river, which was swift and icy cold, many times in the day. The Hunza men, however, are capital and fearless swimmers. Stripping, they plunged into the water and swam on either side of our ponies, holding them up and preventing them from being swept down. In order to reward them, we offered prizes for a swimming contest across the river and back. Their style is a hand-over-hand swimming, and many of the men were carried down at least 300 yards before they succeeded in getting out on the further bank. They also swam with *mussuks*, or inflated goat-skins, lying with their stomachs on the skins and propelling themselves with their hands and feet. By this method in flood-time they bring their women across the river, strapping the lady on to a *mussuk* and swimming at its side themselves. This part of the valley is called Little Guhjal, its inhabitants being Wakhis who originally emigrated from Big Guhjal, or Wakhan, and who still speak the Wakhi language. On the second day we crossed the snout of three glaciers; one of which, the great Pasu glacier, comes striding down to the river's edge with a wilderness of *séracs* and ice-towers, and terminates in a prodigious moraine. On the third day we crossed the Batur glacier, which is a long twisting ice-flood over 20 miles in length. Its surface was split up with lofty pinnacles and crevasses, and we picked our way across in a little over an hour, over ice-hills sprinkled with a black gravelly *débris*. The retrospect was a frozen strait of choppy waves, ridge upon ridge of ice, some snow-white, others as black as soot. This glacier is constantly changing its track, and is sometimes quite impassable.

In this neighbourhood, also, we observed gold-washing on the banks of the river, a man crouching with a wooden trough on a heap of stones by the water's edge, shovelling into it a pile of soil, and then laboriously washing and sifting it out with the aid of a bowl made from a gourd. In this way a few grains are penuriously extracted, and are bought by the Mir with grain, being used by him to pay his annual tribute of 20 ozs. of gold-dust to the Kashmir government, as well as a few *tolas* of gold, which for sake of historical scruples or political expediency, he is still most inexplicably allowed to pay to China.

On the fourth day we passed on the right or west bank of the river the *nullah* that conducts to the difficult Irshad Pass leading to Sarhad, in Wakhan, as well as to the Chilinji Pass, which conducts into the Karumbar valley of Yasin. Of both of these passes, hitherto undescribed and almost unknown, I shall have something to say later on. According to the presence or absence of snow on a particular peak in this part of the main valley do the Hunza people know whether the Irshad Pass is or is not open. A little later we crossed, on the east bank, the deep and narrow gorge down which the Khunjerab river flows from the Khunjerab Pass, leading on to the Taghdumbash Pamir. On the fifth day, following up the valley, which gradually rose, and was filled with clumps of willow and birch in the river's bed, we reached Murkush, just below the junction of the two *nullahs* that conduct respectively to the Kilik and Mintaka Passes, leading on to the same Pamir. Pursuing the former or left hand of these, we camped at an elevation of 13,360 feet (having risen 5300 feet since leaving Baltit), at a few miles from the foot of the Kilik Pass. On the morrow we crossed the latter. I took the elevation on the summit with a boiling-point thermometer, ordinary thermometer, and aneroid, and found it to be 15,870 feet. The top of the Kilik is a long flattish plateau, covered with stones and interspersed with grassy swamps and standing water. There was no snow on the pass itself, though the snow-line was but little above us on the surrounding mountains, which were draped in white. This is the pass of which Captain Grombchevski, who crossed it in August, 1888, penned the somewhat hyperbolic report that it is " exceedingly easy, so that a cart with a full team of horses could follow it." Here we bade goodbye to the Thum of Hunza and his men, the limits of whose jurisdiction we had reached, and were met by the Kirghiz chief of the Taghdumbash Pamir, who is a Chinese subject, and who had received instructions to attend upon us while in Chinese territory. In his company we marched down about 6 miles to our new camp on the Taghdumbash.

Before leaving this portion of the Hindu Kush, or rather of that section of the main range which, extending from this point eastwards to the Karakoram, is locally designated the Mustagh range, let me say an additional word about the passes already mentioned, by which access across it is gained to the Pamirs. They are four in number, viz. in the direction from east to west, the Khunjerab, the Karchenai, the Mintaka, and the Kilik. The Khunjerab Pass[1] was visited on the north side by Captain Younghusband in 1889, and has since been explored by Lieutenant Cockerill. It is a winter pass only, and is all but impracticable for baggage-animals. Its elevation has been determined as 15,420 feet. The Karchenai Pass is reported to be even worse, but is still unknown. Mintaka means the "Pass of a Thousand Ibex," and is also locally called Kirish, i.e. *poshtin*, or sheepskin coat, which name appears in the Russian military topographical map as Kershin. The same map gives the elevation as 15,740 feet. Lieutenant Cockerill made it 15,430 feet; Captain Younghusband, 15,300 feet. It is an easy pass, free from snow in the summer, and practicable for ponies, and is the pass by which Captain Grombchevski rode back from Hunza in 1888 on to the Taghdumbash Pamir. Lastly, as to the several altitudes that have been registered for the Kilik, whereas the Russian map marks it as 16,100 feet, Colonel Woodthorpe, in the Lockhart Mission in 1886, made it 15,600 feet by aneroid; Lieutenant Cockerill, 15,670 feet; myself by hypsometer, 15,870 feet. I would here say, with respect to the varying figures of different authorities, that not merely, as is obvious, must much, if not nearly all, depend upon the nature and reliability of the instrument employed —the aneroid, so far as my own experience goes, being a thoroughly capricious and untrustworthy guide at those elevations—but a good deal of the variation may also be accounted for by the difference of the actual spot in or near to the summit at which the observation is made. When a pass is deep in snow the track is obliterated, and a traveller makes his way across as best he can, and takes his altitude where the position is most favourable. Only when the pass is snow-free can the mathematical summit be accurately determined. It will also have been manifest, from the description of the two passes last named, that while the crossing of the passes themselves is for some five months of the year attended with not the slightest difficulty either for man or beast, the real obstacles are only encountered, and the amazing military strength of the frontier is only ascertained after the passes have been crossed, and the descent begins into the gorges and defiles on their southern side. Crossing the Kilik or the Mintaka is by no means the same thing as getting to Hunza; and I may further add, that getting to Hunza is a very different thing from invading India.

From the summit of the Kilik Pass I looked down upon the first and easternmost of the tracts of country that are called Pamirs; and here, accordingly, I pause to discuss what that name means, how it arose, to what districts it applies, what are the distinctive characteristics, what the hydrography and the orography, and who the inhabitants of

---

[1] This is the pass called Ghundrab in Mohammed Amin's report. *Vide* Davies' 'Report on Trade Routes of the North-West Frontier,' Appendix, p. ccclvi.

tho country so named. To this I shall add a list of the mediæval
travellers who in different ages are known to have visited or traversed
the Pamirs, and a description of the various stages by which that country
has been opened to our knowledge. Finally, I will name the European
travellers who have in recent times penetrated to these little-known
spots for purposes of official exploration, travel, or sport. As regards
the literature of the subject, I need here only mention the writings of
such travellers as have in modern times themselves visited the Pamirs,
and could therefore speak from eye-witness. Of these, five have written
books in the English language : Captain Wood's account of his celebrated
pioneer journey in 1837–8 to the Victoria Lake source of the Oxus ;[1]

NATIVE POLO-PLAYERS.

Sir Thomas Gordon's description of the visit paid to the Pamirs in 1874
by certain members of Sir Douglas Forsyth's second expedition to
Yarkand ;[2] a translation of M. Bonvalot's French work describing his
arduous spring crossing of the Pamirs in 1887 ;[3] (with which may
be compared his companion M. Capus' independent account, in the
French language, of the same journey [4]) ; Lord Dunmore's book ;[5] and
Major Cumberland's narrative of sport on the Eastern Pamirs.[6] Papers

[1] 'A Journey to the Source of the River Oxus.' By Capt. John Wood, I.N. New
edit. London : 1872.
[2] 'The Roof of the World.' By Col. T. E. Gordon. London : 1876.
[3] 'Through the Heart of Asia.' Translated by C. B. Pitman. 2 vols. London : 1889.
[4] ' Le Toit du Monde.' Par G. Capus. Paris : 1890.
[5] 'The Pamirs.' By the Earl of Dunmore. 2 vols. London : 1893.
[6] ' Sport on the Pamirs.' By Major C. S. Cumberland. London : 1895.

have further been communicated to this Society, and have been published in the Journal by certain of the above travellers, viz. by Captain Wood,[1] by Colonel Gordon[2] and Colonel Trotter,[3] (his companion), and by Lord Dunmore,[4] as also by Mr. Littledale,[5] Captain Younghusband,[6] and Captain Bower.[7] To these must be added the invaluable compilations of two writers, in whom the lack of eye-witness was more than compensated by profound scholarship, viz. Sir Henry Rawlinson[8] and Sir Henry Yule.[9] Both, however, wrote at a time when geographical information about the Pamirs was singularly imperfect.

Firstly, as to the name Pamir. Its earliest known occurrence is in the description of the journey of the Chinese Buddhist pilgrim, Hwen Thsang, in the seventh century A.D. He crossed this elevated region and called it Pomilo, a name which resembles the pronunciation Pamil, still reported by some travellers as being used by the Kirghiz at the present day.[10] The same name appears as Pomi in the Chinese Tang history, in reference to the year 747 A.D.[11] Marco Polo, more than 500 years later, called it Pamier. Mirza Haidar, a prince of Kashgar, whose work, the 'Tarikh-i-Rashidi,' written about the year 1543, has recently been edited by Mr. Ney Elias, adopted the modern form, Pamir.[12] The Portuguese Jesuit, Benedict Goez, in 1603 used the phrase Serpanil, which, as Yule suggested, probably signifies Sir-i-pamir, i.e. "Head of the Pamir;" a name closely analogous to the Sir-i-kul, or "Head of the Lake," which was mentioned to Wood in 1838, and mistaken by him for the title of the Great Pamir Lake itself. The Kirghiz whom I met adopted the pronunciation Pâmër rather than Pâmîr. The use of the name, in some form or other, is therefore amply attested for a period of 1200 years.

What, then, is its origin? Here an ample field has been pro-

---

[1] *Journal of the R.G.S.*, vol. x., 1840, p. 530.

[2] *Ibid.*, vol. xlvi., 1876, p. 381.

[3] *Ibid.*, vol. xlviii., 1878, p. 173. *Vide* also Colonel Trotter's report in the published Report of the Forsyth Mission. Calcutta: 1875.

[4] *Geographical Journal*, vol. ii., 1893, p. 385.

[5] *Proceedings of the R.G.S.*, vol. xiv., 1892, p. 1.

[6] *Ibid.*, vol. xiv., 1892, p. 205.

[7] *Geographical Journal*, vol. v., 1895, p. 240.

[8] 'Monograph on the Oxus,' in the *Journal of the R.G.S.*, vol. xlii., 1872, p. 482.

[9] 'Papers connected with the Upper Oxus Region,' in the *Journal of the R.G.S.*, vol. xlii., 1872, p. 438; and Introduction to new edition of Wood's 'Oxus,' 1872.

[10] *E.g.* Fedchenko and Capus (*As. Quart. Rev.*, 1892, p. 238). Marco Polo can hardly, however, have acquired the name, as Prof. Vambéry has suggested, from the Kirghiz, since it was not till the sixteenth century that they came into the Pamirs, being driven southwards by the Kalmuks.

[11] Dr. Bushell, *Journal of the R. As. Soc.*, vol. xii. p. 530.

[12] 'Tarikh-i-Rashidi.' Edited with notes by Ney Elias. London: 1894. *Vide* also a condensed account of the same work by R. B. Shaw, in the *Journal of the R.G.S.*, vol. xlvi., 1876, p. 277.

vided for the ingenuity alike of the amateur philologist and of the student; nor can it be said that the scholarship of the one has carried us much further than the conjectures of the other. The various suggestions may be classified according as the word is supposed to be of Sanskrit, of Turki, or of Persian origin. Under the first heading falls the conjecture of Burnouf,[1] who regarded it as a contraction of *Upa Meru*, i.e. the country above Mount Meru, the legendary holy mountain of Hindu mythology, which was supposed to be the abode of the gods, and the centre of the universe. To the same class belongs Sir H. Rawlinson's conjecture that the word may be a contraction of Fan-mir, or Famir (the Arabic pronunciation), i.e. the lake country of the Fani, or Φαυνοι, who, according to Strabo (Lib. xi. cap. 14), founded the Greek kingdom of Bactria to the east; *mir* being, he says, a Sanskrit word signifying primarily "sea" (e.g. *mare, mer*, and English *mere*), but also "lake," a form which reappears in Kash-mir and Aj-mir.[2] To this theory the objection among others may, I think, reasonably be taken that there is no ground for adopting the Arabic pronunciation, the more so as the name "Pamilo" has been shown to have been in common acceptance long before the Arabs can ever have heard of the word at all. Next comes the Turki school. Colonel Gordon and the members of the Forsyth Mission in 1874 were told by their guides that the word meant "a wilderness, a place depopulated, abandoned, waste, yet capable of habitation." Professor Vambéry has likewise said that it means "a plain or sterile tract of country." For this interpretation I believe there to be no foundation other than the inventiveness of the Kirghiz guides, who, like most cicerones, are not first rate etymologists. Dr. Leitner has said, but I do not know on what authority, that it is a Turki or Yarkandi word meaning "high plain, elevated valley, tableland, or plateau." Major Montgomerie's Mirza suggested the derivation *pa* (belongs), and *mir* (chief), i.e. the territory belonging to the chief of Badakshan, which is, of course, absurd. Finally, there is the school of Persian partisans, whose hypotheses do not in every case err on the side of timidity. By some of these the word Pamir is said to be a contraction of Bam-i-Dunya, or "Roof of the World," another local appellation for the same region, which was mentioned to Wood in 1838. This, I think, is frankly fantastic. Others have suggested Bam-yar, or "Roof of the Earth" (*bam* being a Persian and *yar* a Turki word), which is perhaps worse. Professor Tomaschek, accepting the Aryan origin of the name, mentions other hypothetical Persian roots.[2] Finally comes a series of derivatives of the Persian word *pai*, signifying "foot," and some word of kindred sound to *mir*. Of these the least

---

[1] *Vide* Humboldt's 'Asie Centrale,' vol. i. p. 104; vol. ii. p. 390.

[2] *Journal of the R.G.S.*, vol. xlii., 1872, pp. 489, 496.

[3] 'Centralasiatische Studien II., Pamir Dialecte.' Vienna: 1880.

fanciful, and, if a Persian origin be accepted (as I think it must be,
when we consider that the name was in established usage as early as
the seventh century A.D.), to my mind the most likely, is the combination
pai and *mir*, the latter, whether identical or not with the mythical Meru,
being a word of not uncommon Central Asian use for "mountain,"[1] as,
e.g., Tirich Mir, the famous mountain in the north of Chitral; Deo Mir,
the local name for Nanga Parbat; and Mir Kalan (*i.e.* Big Mountain),
a familiar peak in the Peshawur valley. I should not be so much inclined to identify the Mir in question with any particular peak as to
suppose that the allusion may be to the great ranges—the Trans Alai
on the north, the Mustagh Ata on the east, and the Hindu Kush on the
south by which the Pamir region is ringed, and at whose feet it may
legitimately be said to lie.

I next turn to the physical characteristics of the country so named.
And here I confess that the gravest misconception appears to have
prevailed, and may perhaps even still prevail, in this country as to
what the Pamir or Pamirs really are. Only three years ago they
were described by an eminent English geographer as a "vast tableland." In a leading article in the leading newspaper they have more
recently been said to consist of "a series of bare and storm-swept
downs." The word "steppe" is also of frequent application in popular
parlance. There is quite a remarkable concentration of these errors of
a slipshod nomenclature in a passage in Yule's Introduction to the
second edition of Wood's 'Journey to the source of the Oxus,' published
as recently as 1872. "We know now with something like certainty
that the core of this mountain mass forms a great elevated plateau, the
greatest part of which appears to consist of stretches of tolerably level
steppe, broken and divided by low rounded hills." Elsewhere he writes,
"Mountains in some places lift themselves out of the steppe."

Now, beyond the fact that the general elevation of the Pamir valleys
is from 12,000 to 14,000 feet, and that they are consequently at a higher
level than the surrounding countries, there is nothing in their superficial character in the least degree calculated to suggest a tableland or
plateau, which I take to mean a broad stretch of flat and elevated land,
surrounded, maybe, and even interspersed, but not positively broken up,
with mountain masses. Nor can anything less like a down or a steppe be
conceived than the troughs or valleys, of no great width, shelving downwards to a river-bed or lake, and uniformly framed on either hand by
mountains whose heads are perpetually covered with snow, which
anybody who has been to the Pamirs will at once recognize as a fair
description of those regions. In reality, over the entire region embraced
by the title, it has been calculated that the plains or valleys constitute
less than one-tenth of the total area. Correctly described, a Pamir in

[1] In Baber's 'Memoirs' (translated by Leyden and Erskine), p. 313, *Mir* is said to
mean a hill.

theory, and each Pamir in fact, is therefore neither a plain nor a down, nor a steppe, nor a plateau, but a mountain valley of glacial formation, differing only from the adjacent or other mountain valleys in its superior altitude, and in the greater degree to which its trough has been filled up by glacial detritus and alluvium, and has thereby approximated in appearance to a plain owing to the inability of the central stream to scour for itself a deeper channel; this inability again being attributable to the width of the valleys and the consequent absence of glaciers on any scale, and to the short summers, which do not last long enough or experience a sufficiently fierce sun to admit of a very powerful erosive impetus being communicated to the melting snow.   The northern Pamirs, notably those near Rang Kul, Tagharma, and the Western Alichur, are flatter and more open than those on the southern fringe of the region.

BAND AND SPECTATORS ON POLO GROUND.

Every Pamir, then, that I saw possessed the same characteristics associated with a greater or less width.   These were—the bordering presence of successive mountain peaks, snow-crowned above, sometimes seamed with ice-fields, and terminating in steep shingle slopes or boulder-strewn undulations lower down; in the bottom of the valley a river or stream or mountain torrent, noisily spreading itself over a stony bed or meandering in a peaty track, and sometimes feeding a lake or succession of lakes; and on either bank of the stream or lake a more or

B

less level expanse of spongy soil, usually covered with a coarse yellow grass, and frequently broken up by swampy patches exactly like the ground on a Scottish moor. With the grassy stretches, which are green and flower-bestrewn in the summer only, and during the rest of the year—when not covered with snow—are sere and yellow, are interspersed expanses of sand and clay and stones, very often overlaid with a powdery incrustation of magnesium (where the saline properties in the soil have become exhausted) that glitters like a hoar-frost in the sun.

The main and differentiating features, therefore, of a Pamir are the abundance of pasturage, affording excellent food for every variety of animal; and the almost total absence either of timber or of cultivation. There are parts of the Pamirs where a few trees grow, and where a scant tillage is practised;[1] but these are not sufficiently numerous to invalidate the general proposition which I have stated. Hence it arises that such opposite verdicts have been passed by different travellers upon the fertility or reverse of the Pamirs. Those who expect some sort of forest growth, some signs of plantation, natural or artificial, or some evidences of settled human habitation, have, on finding none of these, denounced in savage terms the sullen inhospitality of the scene. Those, on the other hand, who have seen either their own animals or the Kirghiz flocks grow fat upon the succulent Pamir grass have spoken in glowing terms of these mountain pastures. The fact is that the Pamirs are both fertile and barren, both habitable and desolate, both smiling and repellent, according to the point of view from which they are regarded. They are among the deliberate paradoxes of nature.

It is owing to the climatic conditions under which this peculiar region subsists that the unfavourable verdict has on the whole prevailed. Possessing a mean elevation of from 12,000 to 14,000 feet above the sea, with peaks that rise to 20,000 feet and higher, buried deep in snow during seven months of the year, and often inaccessible for a much longer time, scourged by icy blasts, destitute of any fuel,

---

[1] These are in the adjoining valleys rather than on the Pamirs themselves. Ivanoff mentions a forest growth consisting of creepers, reeds, rose, willow, dwarf birch, mountain poplar, bramble, liquorice root, honeysuckle, spurge, and black currant; but the traveller will certainly meet with few or none of these on the ordinary Pamirs. He also says that barley and wheat are sometimes cultivated; but this has not been the experience of the Russian garrison of the Murghabi fort or Pamirski Poste, who, during the few years of their occupation, have attempted, with little or no success, to grow potatoes, radishes, and other vegetables. The poverty of the resources is really, however, best indicated by the paucity of inhabitants. In 1892 the *Turkestan Gazette* said that the only permanent population of the Pamirs consisted of 250 *kibitkas* or 1500 Kirghiz, and these of inferior breed and stamina. Their number is said now to have fallen to 1000. A previous number of this Journal (February, 1893, p. 159) contained an extract from a lecture delivered at Moscow in January, 1893, by a Spanish traveller, M. Ximénès, on his alleged recent travels in the Pamirs, in the course of which he said, " The magnificent pasture-lands of the Pamirs afford nourishment to herds of superb cattle and excellent mountain horses." M. Ximénès, however, I have reason to believe, was never nearer to the Pamirs than Tashkend.

save that which is provided by the dung of animals or the roots of desert scrub, and devoid of the meanest consolations of life, it is not surprising that the Roof of the World has been generally voted one of its least desirable portions, and until quite recent times, when fresh reasons were discovered for its examination, has been tacitly excluded from the itinerary of the most intrepid of explorers. That, however, is no reason why we should call it what it is not, or perpetuate the errors of a more ignorant time.

There are eight claimants to the distinction and title of a Pamir, whose pretensions appear to be sufficiently established by local usage, though it is a mistake to suppose that the nomad Kirghiz will at once in each case recognize them by the accepted geographical name. They are as follows:—

1. The Taghdumbash, or Supreme Head of the Mountains Pamir. This is the Pamir lying immediately below and to the north of the Kilik Pass. It is closed on the west by the valley leading up to the Wakh-jir pass into Wakhan, from which point it first stretches away in an easterly direction to Ujad-bai, where it receives a second fork or bay coming from the direction of the Khunjerab Pass on the south, and then turns north, till it finally terminates at the Chinese fort of Tashkurghan, a total distance of about 60 miles. This Pamir lies in a different watershed from the whole of the remaining Pamirs, and is physically, as well as politically, part of a different system. Its elevation ranges from 10,000 feet at its northern to 15,000 feet at its western extremity, and its breadth varies from 1 to 5 miles. Its inhabitants are Kirghiz, Sarikolis, and occasionally a few fugitives from Wakhan. They are under the jurisdiction of China, whose authority is represented by sixty soldiers in the fort at Tashkurghan, and who is as ignorant of the real conditions in her Pamir dominions, and as utterly incapable of defending them, as she has recently been proved to be in places that are the keys of the empire and under the very eye of the central government. At the time of my visit the Kirghiz head-man, who was responsible to the Chinese for the local jurisdiction, was Kasim Beg, who, with his family and flocks, was a fugitive from the more westerly Pamirs that had been occupied by Russia. He has since resigned the post.

2. The second Pamir is the Pamir-i-Wakhan, a narrow strip of grassy valley extending upon the northern bank of the Ab-i-Wakhan, or head stream of the Oxus, for about 20 miles from some distance below its source down to Bozai Gumbaz. It is the narrowest of all the Pamirs, and is entirely uninhabited, but contains excellent grazing on the slopes.

3. The third is the Pamir-i-Khurd, or Little Pamir, which begins on the south in the valley of the Sarhad branch of the Oxus, a little above Bozai Gumbaz, encloses Lake Chakmak and then runs in a north-easterly direction upon either bank of the Aksu river to the destroyed and evacuated Chinese fort of Aktash. Its total length up to this point is about 60 miles, and it is here separated by a mountain range of no

considerable breadth, crossed by the Neza Tash pass (14,920 feet) from
the head of the Taghdumbash Pamir and the rival watershed of Chinese
Turkistan.   This Pamir varies from 1 to 4 miles in width.   Though it
is commonly regarded as terminating at Aktash, the valley continues
with very much the same characteristics in a north-west direction,
towards the junction of the Aksu river with the Ak-baital—an almost
identical distance—but local caprice seems never to have invested it in
this part with the title of a Pamir.

4. The fourth Pamir, as its name implies, is both in length and
width the most considerable of all. This is the Pamir-i-Kalan, or Great
Pamir, which commences on the south-west at a point below Yol Mazar,
in the valley of the Pamir River branch of the Oxus, first explored by
Wood, and then runs in an easterly direction, containing Wood's or
Victoria Lake, and the small chain of lakes at its eastern extremity,
and extending for a total length of about 80 miles as far as the watershed of the Aksu.   Its width varies from 1 to 6 miles.

5. Continuing to the north, we next come to the Alichur Pamir,
reaching on the west to the borders of Shighnan, drained by a river
of the same name, and including the chain of lakes known as Yeshil
Kul or Green Lake, Bulun Kul, and Sasik Kul or Putrid Lake.   This
Pamir is separated on the north by a lofty range of mountains from the
next adjoining basin of the Murghab or Aksu.

6. In the watershed of the latter there appears on several maps, and
there has been reported by more than one traveller as existing, the
Sarez Pamir.   In so far as the name is associated with that portion of
the valley of the Murghab near Sarez, it has been pointed out by Mr.
Ney Elias that it is a misnomer, since the valley there is very mountainous, and has none of the characteristics of a Pamir.   Captain
Younghusband, however, gives the name to a small piece of more open
and grassy valley about 10 miles long below the Russian fort of
Murghabi, from which it would appear that the title has been shifted
to some distance from the original Sarez.[1]

7, 8. The seventh and eighth Pamirs may be more rapidly dis-
missed.   They are the Rang Kul Pamir, containing the lake of that
name, which was formerly a Chinese but is now a Russian possession ;
and the Khargosh or Hare Pamir, which contains the basin of the Great
Kara Kul Lake, and lies along the valley of the small stream that flows
into it from the south, and along its eastern shore.

These are the main and authentic Pamirs.   There are various other
stretches of country to which the name has sometimes been applied,

---

[1] The Sarez Pamir was first reported by Pundit Manphul in 1867 (Davies' 'Re-
port on Trade-Routes of the North-West Frontier,' Appendix, p. cccxxxii.). Colonel
Gordon in 1874 speaks of the "Siriz Pamir as a continuation of the Aktash valley from
Akbalik (i.e. the junction of the Aksu and Ak-baital) westwards to Bartang, the
commencement of inhabited Shighnan, on the west" ('Roof of the World,' p. 158).
Colonel Trotter on his map called it Sariz Pamir, but spelt Sirich Fort.

but to which it cannot be considered indisputably to appertain. These are, on the western side of the recorded Pamirs, the Pamir-i-Bugrumal, a valley below Yeshil Kul near the head of the Ghund valley, which was mentioned by Colonel Trotter; and on the eastern side, the Mariom or Marian Pamir,[1] which is depicted on some maps as an easterly branch of the Taghdumbash Pamir; and further, again, to the north the Sarikol Pamir. Sarikol, however, is not a Pamir, but a district, and the title is therefore a misnomer. It has also been said that the country lying on the Sarikol side of the Shimshal Pass in the Mustagh range, by which the Kanjutis used to make their raids upon the Yarkand-Leh caravans, is

HEAD OF THE KUKTURUK NULLAH.

called by them the Shimshal Pamir.[2] Colonel Gordon further spoke of the Shiwa Pamir in Badakshan.[3] In each of these cases the appellation, even if based upon physical resemblances, seems to be supported by insufficient evidence or usage, and cannot therefore be sustained.

As to the total area of the Pamirs proper, Sir H. Yule said that the plateau, as he called it, was at least 180 miles from north to south, and something like 100 miles from east to west. Mr. Freshfield, at a meeting of this Society in 1892, gave the figures as 280 miles of length

---

[1] It is called Maryang, and is described as a *kishlak* or *taluka* in the Uchi valley of the province of Tashkurghan, by Mohammed Amin, in Davies' Report, Appendix, p. cccxxix.

[2] *Vide* Biddulph's 'Tribes of the Hindu Kush,' p. 26.

[3] 'Roof of the World,' p. 162.

by 120–150 miles of breadth. I calculate that the extreme length and breadth are almost exactly equal, and I reckon both at 150 miles, as measured by a compass upon the map.

I have already alluded to nomad Kirghiz as almost the sole inhabitants of the Pamirs. They are supplemented in a few places by wandering camps of Wakhis, Sarikolis, and Tajiks from Shighnan; but the population is kept down by the inability of the women to bear large families in so arduous a climate. With their flocks of sheep and goats, and droves of ponies and yaks, these nomads roam about, pitching their camps where the grass is best or the cold least severe. The bulk of the Kirghiz have at different times acknowledged a sort of general allegiance to China, as till lately the greatest neighbouring Power. Others have been subordinate to the Afghans, whom, however, they appear not to like. They are in reality ready to side with any power and to profess any allegiance that will least compromise their own independence. The Russians, since their appearance on the Pamirs, have claimed to exercise a sort of general suzerainty over the Kirghiz, on the ground that they were subjects of the annexed Khanate of Kokand; to which several of the tribes have replied by emigrating across the border into what is admittedly Chinese territory. I know of no foundation, historical or ethnological, for the claim, no mention of which is made by any of the Russian historians of Kokand (Nazaroff, Khoroshkin, and Nalivkin), while other Russian writers (e.g. Zagriashki and Radloff) have unreservedly acknowledged the Kirghiz allegiance to China.

I need not say much about the Pamir climate. It is widely known that for six if not seven months of the year, and certainly from the middle of November to the end of April, the Pamirs are deeply covered with snow, the lakes are frozen, and the passes are well-nigh impassable. The experience of the French travellers, Messrs. Bonvalot, Capus, and Pepin, who crossed the entire region from north to south in April, 1887, gives a fair indication of what may then be expected. On the other hand, at their entrenched encampment of Murghabi or Pamirski Poste, situated at the junction of the Aksu and Ak-baital rivers, at an elevation of 12,150 feet, we know that 200 Russians have now been stationed throughout the winter for nearly three years. They are reported to have suffered severe hardships, but are well accommodated and housed.[1] The Kirghiz detest the neighbourhood of Lake Victoria, and will never voluntarily encamp there, saying that the climate gives them pain in

---

[1] Since the Russians were installed at Murghabi, lat. 38° 8′, long. (from Pulkowa) 43° 37′, an opportunity has been offered, for the first time in history, of making continuous meteorological observations on the Pamirs. The Paris Geographical Society published in its *Comptes Rendus*, No. 1, 1895, the following table, which contains an entire year's observations, from September, 1893, to September, 1894. I have converted the Centigrade into Fahrenheit scale.

the throat and chest. Their women find great difficulty in child-bearing on the Pamirs, the offspring being usually stillborn. Similarly, at Pamirski Poste the Russians have been unable to keep poultry alive, and have found that dogs will only breed once in three years. In the more southerly Pamirs the chief drawback to comfort is the wind, which usually blows with cutting intensity at some time in the day, and is worse than the cold. In Wakhan there is a particularly vicious wind, named the Bad-i-Wakhan, which blows steadily down the valley of the Oxus without intermission for weeks at a time, but sometimes takes the opposite direction. When I was on the Pamirs in September and October, the temperature, though it commonly sank to below zero (Fahr.) in the night or early morning, was delightful as soon as the sun was high. The air was crisp and invigorating, and, except when the wind was blowing, a more exhilarating climate could not be conceived. I did not myself feel the rarefaction of the air at all seriously below 16,500 feet; but our camp-followers, notably those who had come from India, were affected at a considerably lower level.

As regards the fauna of the Pamirs, I may refer for birds to the well-known paper of Severtsoff (translated in The *Ibis* of 1883). He mentions 120 different species, some breeding in the Pamirs, others only migratory, but none absolutely peculiar to the region. I saw myself wild geese and wild-fowl of many descriptions on the lakes. There were also snipe ; I shot a quail at an elevation of nearly 14,000 feet on the northern slopes of the Chakmak Lake, and I saw them at 15,000 feet on

Year.	Month.			Mean temperature, Fahr.	Mean nebulosity, per cent.	Rainfall, millimetres.	Prevailing wind.
1893	September	...	...	47°	32	2·0	S.W.
	October	...	...	30°	22	0·0	S.W.
	November	...	...	17°	30	0·1	S.W.
	December	...	...	9°	47	4·2	S.W.
1894	January	...	...	−13°	56	2·8	S.W.
	February	...	...	0°	50	0·9	S.W.
	March	...	...	22°	44	0·7	N.E.
	April	...	...	34°	44	9·4	N.E.
	May	...	...	42°	42	12·4	N.E.
	June	...	...	54°	35	4·7	N.E.
	July	...	...	62°	50	11·3	N.E.
	August	...	...	56°	19	0·0	—

During the above period the minimum temperature recorded was −47° Fahr. in January, and the maximum 82° Fahr. in July. It froze in the morning during every month of the year. The rainfall is the lowest in the entire Russian Empire, seven times less than at Tashkend, and twice less than at Khiva. The north-east winds are much more violent than the south-west, and frequently culminate in hurricanes. In August there is a sort of equilibrium, and the winds blow equally from all points of the compass. Then also the sky is most clear. For some further information on the meteorology of the Pamirs, *vide* M. Capus' notes published in the Bulletin of the Paris Geographical Society, 1892, p. 316.

the Taghdumbash Pamir. Lord Dunmore saw the common seagull on
Victoria Lake. *Chikor*,[1] a bird resembling the French partridge, are very
numerous in the Oxus valley, and snow-cocks or snow-pheasants have
been frequently reported.[2] I saw eagles and lammergeier overhead.
Hares positively swarm on the Taghdumbash, hopping about among the
rocks and stones. There were also numbers of grey or silver foxes, scurry-
ing from burrows in the sandy soil, and a species of marmot. Colonel
Gordon also mentions the lynx. Fish are very plentiful in the lakes, and
many of the streams swarm with a species of carp. Among the larger
fauna, brown, red, and grey bears, snow-leopards and ibex are encountered
in the mountains ; Dr. Potagos, in 1870, encountered a species of troglo-
dyte ape near Sarhad ; and wolves and wild dogs chase the *Ovis Poli* over
the snowy ridges. The latter animal, or celebrated ram of the Pamirs,
is, of course, the chief glory of the region, whilst, owing to the extreme
remoteness of its haunts, it still remains the most cherished object of the
modern sportsman's ambition. So little information of any scientific value
is, however, to be found about it in the English language, that I am
tempted to add here the results of my own investigations.

The *Ovis Poli* is only one, though the largest and most famous, of a
group of wild sheep that are found in many localities over a wide range
in Central Asia, constituting a *genus*, the distinction of whose individual
species still lacks scientific determination. Of these the *Ovis Poli, Ovis
Karelini* (so named from the Russian explorer, Karelin, who was the
first to obtain a specimen in the Ala Tau near Semirechinsk, in about
1840), *Ovis Heinsii, Ovis Nigrimontana*, and *Ovis Argali*, have been
separately named ; the only authority who has devoted a first-hand
and exhaustive inquiry to the subject being the Russian naturalist,
Severtsoff.[3] The *Ovis Poli* and *Ovis Karelini*, however, share a large
number of characteristics, which differentiate them to some extent from
the remaining species.

The *Ovis Poli* was first so named by Blyth (in compliment to its
original description by Marco Polo), from a head sent home by Captain

[1] This is the small *chikor*, or Himalayan red-legged partridge (*Caccabis Chukor* of
Gray) which Moorcroft in his travels mistook for the francolin.

[2] The snow-cock (*Tretraogallus Himalayensis* of Gray) is identical with the larger
chikor, a bird as big as a hen-turkey, described by Moorcroft and Vigne, and frequently
mentioned to me in the Hindu Kush region, though I never encountered it. Its
Kashmiri and Himalayan name is *koklas*, its Ladaki (*i.e.* Tibetan) title *ribcha*.

[3] His treatise on the 'Mammals of Turkestan,' translated from the *Trans. of the
Imp. Soc. of Naturalists of Moscow*, vol. viii., 1873, appeared in the *Annals and Magazine
of Natural History*, vol. xvii., 4th series, 1876, pp. 171, 210, 217–220, 220–226. In the
Proceedings of the Zoological Society of London have also been printed a number of
papers by English writers, viz. Blyth, 1840, p. 62 ; P. L. Sclater, 1860, p. 443 ; Colonel
Gordon and Dr. Stoliczka, 1874, pp. 53, 425 ; Captain Biddulph, 1875, p. 157 ; Sir V. Brooke
and B. Brooke, 1875, p. 509 ; W. T. Blanford, 1884, p. 326. The majority of these
relate to the *Ovis Poli*. For accounts by sportsmen of the pursuit of the latter animal,
vide St. G. Littledale, cap. xii. vol. ii. of 'Big Game Shooting,' in the Badminton
Library ; and Lord Dunmore and Major Cumberland in the books before cited.

Wood from Lake Victoria in 1838. Wood misnamed the animal *kutch-kar*, whereas Blyth identified the *ras* or *roosh*, mentioned by Burnes, with the *Ovis Poli*. The Kirghiz name, which I always heard employed, was *gulcha* or *gulja* for the male, and *arkar* for the female. The latter is a smaller animal, and has short horns, lying rather backward.

It is for his magnificent horns, of immense thickness, extraordinary length, wide span, and, in the case of the older rams, double convolution, that the male is specially renowned. The biggest head known to exist is one that had been picked up (not shot), and was presented to Lord Roberts by the Maharaja of Kashmir. Its length from base to tip of the horn is 75 inches; circumference of horn at the base, 16 inches; width of horns from tip to tip, 54½ inches. The recent Boundary Commission measured a single horn of a broken skull, which was lying in a heap at the mouth of the Urta Bel pass, and found it 72 inches. The largest head in the Natural History Museum at Kensington measures 68 inches in the horn, and is from the collection of the late Mr. A. Dalgleish. The biggest head that has fallen to the rifle is 65 inches. The horns are ringed by well-marked indentations or annulations, corresponding to the age of the animal; although it is only the minimum age that can be determined, since the original rings get blunted and worn away as they grow towards the extremity. Enormous numbers of skulls and of broken or rotting horns are strewn all about the Pamirs, and are often collected by the Kirghiz in heaps. Judging from their extraordinary abundance, the mortality arising from attacks by wolves and wild dogs, from the severity of the climate, and from combats among the males, must be very great.[1] The breeding season of the females begins in October.

The locality in which *Ovis Poli* have been chiefly, if not solely, encountered by Englishmen, is the Pamirs. Throughout the region between the Great Kara Kul and the southern boundary of the Taghdumbash Pamir they are found in large herds. I did not myself observe more than fifteen or twenty in a herd, but as many as three hundred were seen by the recent Boundary Commission at one time. Their *habitat*, however, is by no means confined to the Pamirs, which are merely the south-west corner of their range. Severtsoff says they were met by Semenoff in great abundance on the high plains of Aksai, and of Khan Tengri in the Tian Shan mountains, and about the sources of the rivers Karkara, Tekes, and Sarijazin, to the east and south-east of Issik Kul. From here their range extends in a south-westerly direction to the Narin, the upper Sir Daria, and the tributaries of the Kashgar Daria, *i.e.* as far as the Alai. The lowest elevation, however, at which Severtsoff or Semenoff reported them was about 10,000 feet. The *Ovis*

---

[1] The story is told of the *Ovis Poli*, as of other mountain sheep, that, when jumping, the excessive weight of the horns sometimes makes the ram lose his balance and pitch on to his head. But I doubt if there is any foundation for this tale.

Poli may be said, therefore, to have a double *habitat*, the western Tian Shan and the Pamirs, separated from each other by the Great Alai.

Here, however, we are met by the as yet unsolved problem of the precise identity of the brother sheep, or *Ovis Karelini*. The latter was shot by Forsyth's and Gordon's party in 1872, in the western Tian Shan, to the north-west of Kashgar. They thought it the same as the *Ovis Poli*, though it had smaller horns; but later on, when they compared the two species at Calcutta, they thought them distinct. Undoubtedly there are superficial differences of a marked character, which render the majority of specimens easy of distinction. These differences may be thus summarized :

Ovis Poli.	Ovis Karelini.

Habitat.

The range of *O. P.* has already been mentioned. At one place, viz. Ulan, above the mountains of Atpash, Severtsoff found *O. P.* and *O. K.* living together.	*O. K.* has not been met with in the Pamirs. It is very plentiful, however, in the Semirechinsk province, north of Issik Kul, in the Altai and Sapliski Altai, and in the mountains and plains between the rivers Chilik and Keben, east of Turgeli; and its range is partly identical with, partly to the north-ward of, that of *O. P.*

Elevation.

O. P. has not yet been reported at a lower elevation than 10,000 feet, but is encountered up to 17,000 feet.	*O. K.* is found at every elevation from 2000 to 12,000 feet.

Size of Animal.

O. P. is a larger animal. Severtsoff gave the average height at shoulder as 3 feet 10 inches, average length as 6 feet 7 inches.	Average height of *O. K.* at shoulder is 3 feet 6 inches; average length, 5 feet 10 inches to 6 feet.

Colour of Neck and Mane.

O. P. has a much longer and whiter mane, which is 3 to 4 inches long on the spine, and 6 to 7 inches on the throat and neck.	There is more brown and grey hair in the mane of *O. K.*, which is also shorter.

Length of Horns.

Herein lies the main difference. The horns of *O. P.* are more than four times the length of its skull. Longest recorded horn, 75 inches.	*O. K.*'s horns are only three times the length of its skull. Longest recorded horn, 48½ inches.

Span and Curve of Horns.

O. P.'s horns have a much wider span, and branch further away from the head. In the case of the older rams, they also describe the beautiful twofold outward curve.

O. K.'s horns are set closer on the head, describe a narrower sweep, and (so far as I have seen) never attain the double twist.

These are the main superficial differences between the majority of the observed specimens of the two sheep. On the other hand, there occurs a point at which even these salient characteristics appear to blend, and at which no immutable difference is left between them. In other words, the abnormal *Ovis Poli* can scarcely be distinguished from the normal *Ovis Karelini,* nor the abnormal *Ovis Karelini* from the normal *Ovis Poli.* Hence it has been contended by Mr. Blanford and others that to speak of them as belonging to different species is erroneous. Perhaps it would be safer at this stage to say that the examination of a much larger number of specimens coming from a much wider area than is accessible, at any rate to the English student, is required, before the latter can arrive at any scientific induction. St. Petersburg would probably afford better materials for such a scrutiny than London. In our Natural History Museum *Ovis Karelini* is labelled as a variety of *Ovis Poli,* because of the prior discovery of the latter.

The mention of Marco Polo's sheep brings me back to the point at which I left my own journey to embark upon a general digression on the Pamirs. This was near the westerly termination of the Taghdumbash Pamir. There the Kirghiz had pitched for us three of those circular huts of felt, spread over a wickerwork frame, which are variously called *akoi* (*i.e.* white house) and *yourt* by the Kirghiz, *kibitka* (a Tartar word) by the Russians, *alachik* by the Turkomans, *gor* by the Mongols, and *kirgah* (*i.e.* warm place) by the Afghans. In cold regions like the Pamirs they are incomparably better and more comfortable than any tent. A fire can be lit inside, and the amount of ventilation and degree of warmth can be regulated by pulling the felt coverings on or off the roof. During my subsequent march through Afghanistan in December from Kabul to Chaman, I invariably slept in a *kirgah* lent me by the Amir. The Russian soldiers, in their fort at Murghabi on the Pamirs, are similarly installed.[1] On

[1] The lower part of the hut is made of a framework of willow sticks, which, when pulled out and fixed, covers a diameter of about 14 feet. These constitute the outer walls, and are covered outside with reed mats and felts, which are sometimes kept in place by richly embroidered needlework belts. On to the top of this framework, which is 5 feet in height, are tied curving willow rods, which converge upwards towards the roof, where a circular aperture is left nearly 5 feet across, further transverse oziers forming an open dome, over which the roof-felts are pulled by outside cords. The total height from floor to apex is from 10 to 12 feet.

the Taghdumbash, Lennard and I devoted four days to stalking *Ovis Poli* in the neighbouring *nullahs*. Of these the favourite one for European sportsmen, and the spot where the bulk of the large heads have so far been obtained, is the Kukturuk *nullah*, which runs for a distance of between 4 or 5 miles between lofty mountains in a north and north-westerly direction from the Pamir. A stream courses along a stony bed in the bottom of the valley, which is not more than a quarter to half a mile wide. At its upper end stands a curious mountain with a pointed summit like a tooth (which appears in the photograph printed on p. 21), to the right and left of which the valley splits into two smaller *nullahs*, which are presently blocked with snow. I was lucky enough,

AKOI, OR YOURT.

in the course of only two days' stalking in the Kukturuk, to get two heads, though the dimensions of the larger of these, 54 inches along the outer rim of the horns from the base to the tip, could not be compared with the big heads of 60 inches and upwards that have been shot by Littledale, Lennard, and other sportsmen. The fact is, that so circumscribed is the area, not in which the *Ovis Poli* exists, but in which it has hitherto been procurable by British sports-men, and so serious have been the depredations made by recent visitors upon the accessible herds within this area, that there is already a sensible diminution in the number of first-class heads that are seen ; and unless some measures are adopted to regulate the exuberant zeal of the hunters who take advantage of passports to Chinese Turkestan to decimate the resources of the Taghdumbash Pamir, the time cannot be far distant when the finest of these magnificent animals, instead of peering from their native retreats in the Kukturuk *nullah*, will only be visible behind a glass case in European museums. It is nothing less than an absurdity that, while English officers and travellers are prohibited by the Indian Government from crossing the Hindu Kush for fear of exciting Russian susceptibilities on the Pamirs, they should be able to arrive at exactly the same destination and to inspire the self-same alarms, whether real or hypothetical, at the same time that they render such an ill service to genuine sport, by adopting the circuitous route of the Karakoram and Yarkand. If some sensible restriction, however, be placed both upon the facilities afforded to travellers, and upon the number of heads that they are permitted to kill, there is no reason why the famous ram of the Pamirs should not remain the supreme and legitimate object of the sportsman's desire for many years to come. I should add that we were on the ground at the wrong time of the year for sport. All the big bags have been made in the late spring and early summer, when there is still plenty of snow, and the rams come down to feed upon the young grass that is then springing by the streams. No severe climbing is at that season required in their pursuit; the animals furnish very easy shots, and their retreat is frequently impeded by the depth of the snow. In the late autumn, on the other hand, they spend the greater part of the day above the snow-line and on the topmost peaks. In my own case I had to climb after them through the snow to an elevation of approximately 17,000 feet, at which the difficulty of respiration was very great.

From the Taghdumbash we crossed the Wakh-jir Pass to the watershed of the Oxus and the Wakhan Pamir. The Wakh-jir valley opens out at the extreme westerly end of the Taghdumbash. It has two forks, over the pass that closes the more southerly of which Captain Younghusband made his way with yaks in October, 1891, to the Upper Oxus valley. The right fork is that which leads to the Wakh-jir Pass. This appeared to be the name by which it is known to the Kirghiz; Khujrui, I was told, being the title given to it by the people of Sarhad and Wakhan. The name Wakhjrui, which I see printed upon many maps, I take, therefore, to be a confusion of the two names.[1] The ascent is gradual, but there is a steep rise in the latter part towards a lake about 1000 yards long by 250 yards broad, which is fed by a small stream at its westerly end, and itself discharges the Wakh-jir tributary

---

[1] The pass is called Karanchunkar in the report of Mohammed Amin of Yarkand, Adolph Schlagintweit's guide. *Vide* Davies' 'Report on Trade Routes,' 1862, Appendix iv. B. This is the same name as Karachukur, the name given by Grombchevski and the Russians to the upper course of the Taghdumbash stream. As applied to a pass, it appears more strictly to belong to a *nullah* leading from the Taghdumbash to the Little Pamir, to the east of the Kukturuk.

to the Danga-bash or Taghdumbash river from its eastern extremity. A short sharp rise conducts to a flat stony plateau which is the summit of the pass. I broke my last remaining thermometer while taking the altitude by boiling-point on the summit. The Russian map gives it as 15,070 feet, M. Dauvergne by aneroid as 15,600 feet, Colonel Woodthorpe by hypsometer as 16,150 feet, the Indian Intelligence map as 17,000 feet, and Lord Dunmore by aneroid as 17,200 feet. All purely aneroid measurements are to be distrusted. My own aneroid, as soon as I got above 13,000 feet, performed the most ridiculous freaks, which their intrinsic absurdity compels me to suppress.

From the top of the Wakh-jir Pass the descent is rather steep and stony towards the Oxus valley, which is visible far down below, a blue line of shingle-bed winding away between lofty ridges crowned with snow, particularly on the south bank. As this is the stream which I believe, and shall here argue to be the true and indisputable source of the Oxus, I will first describe my visit to the actual spot, and will then deploy the line of reasoning by which its claims are sustained. Though the former involves but a divergence of a few miles from the track, and though the glacier or glaciers from which the river springs are visible at the head of the valley, no traveller that I am aware of has taken the trouble to ride up to the place itself. M. Dauvergne, who camped at a little distance in 1889, and who, as Colonel Woodthorpe had already done in 1886, rightly concluded that this was the parent stream, drew a picture of three great glaciers.[1] They also appear as such in the Russian military map, which coolly calls them the Baron Vrevski glacier, from the name of the present Governor-General of Russian Turkestan. The Indian and English Intelligence maps represent quite a number of parallel glaciers. The only map in which their position and shape are at all accurately rendered is that of the native surveyor who accompanied the mission of Lockhart and Woodthorpe in 1886, but of which there is not a copy in England. I will describe what are the actual facts.

From far above, the main glacier can be seen winding round from the north or left hand to the head of the gorge, in which, however, its point of discharge is not visible. Descending to the shingle-bed, which varies from 100 to 350 yards in width, the channel being divided into several branches of from 6 to 18 inches deep, I rode up it to the source. There the river issues from two ice-caverns in a rushing stream. The cavern on the right has a low overhanging roof, from which the water gushes tumultuously out. The cavern on the left was sufficiently high to admit of my looking into the interior, and within for some distance I could follow the river, which was blocked with great slabs of ice,

---

[1] *Vide* his paper published in the Bulletin of the French Geog. Soc. for 1892, and condensed in *Proceedings of the R.G.S.*, vol. xiv., 1892, p. 779, and in the *Scottish Geog. Mag.*, 1892, p. 362. He gave the elevation of his camp as 14,700 feet, and the position as lat. 37° 10', long. 75° E.

while there was a ceaseless noise of grinding, crunching, and falling in. Above the ice-caves is the precipitous front wall or broken snout of the glacier, from 60 to 80 feet in height, composed of moraine ice, covered with stones and black dust. I clambered up this to the level of the top of the moraine, and from there could see the big glacier, with its jagged ice-towers and pinnacles and crevasses coming down from a valley on the left. A lofty mountain crowned with snow blocked up the end of the main valley, and from a *nullah* on the right of this, another ice-field contributed its volume to the main glacier, whose terminal moraine was jammed up and contracted in the narrow outlet of the two valleys. The

HEAD OF OVIS POLI.

source of the river is, therefore, not in three great glaciers, but in one great glacier, to which smaller glaciers contribute. At a short distance below the source, a small but incomplete glacier comes to the edge of the cliff on the southern bank, and no doubt frequently adds to the volume of the stream. When I saw it, no water was issuing from its base. When Captain Younghusband, in 1891, crossed over the more southerly fork of the Wakh-jir Pass, as before mentioned, and was on the Oxus slope of the watershed, he came upon a small lake, from which issued a tricklet of water.[1] This, no doubt, was one of the feeders of the big glacier which I have described.

---

[1] Vide *Proceedings of the R.G.S.*, vol. xiv., 1892, p. 231.

Now, before I proceed to state why this is the chief source of the Oxus, let me name, in order of their occurrence, the names of all the claimants to the title. The stream whose source I have depicted is called the Wakh-jir, from the pass which I had crossed, and from the west end of which three rills trickle down the mountain-side and fall into its bed a few miles below the glacier. This name erroneously appears as Varjer in Mr. Littledale's paper and map.[1] Lord Dunmore calls this the Ak Bilis, or White Pass or col, but I know not on what authority. The name appears on no map, and, so far as I know, has never previously been heard of or mentioned by any traveller. None of the Kirghiz or other people with me had ever heard of such a title. Some maps, including both the Indian and English Intelligence maps, call this branch the Aimagon or Almaghan; and M. Capus, perhaps from such a map, spoke of the pass as the Akdjir (obviously Wakh-jir) or Almaiane. The same name appears as Almagan in the published report of Ivanoff and Benderski's great expedition in 1883, and as Almayan-saya in Grombchevski's report in 1889. What this word may mean has always been to me a mystery. I could gather nothing about it on the spot. It has been suggested that it may have arisen from the blunder of some careless copyist or compositor, who mistook the letters of the name Ab-i-Wakhan, which the river undoubtedly bears lower down. But this hardly seems to explain its appearance in so many independent quarters. M. Capus also mentions the name Ab-i-Chipri, but this again is quite without confirmation, unless, perhaps, it be a perversion of Ab-i-Chap, i.e. the left-hand stream.

The next claimant is the stream, perhaps best called the Sarhad or Little Pamir stream, which flows into the Wakh-jir at Bozai Gumbaz, about 25 miles below the glacier source, and which itself rises in the low col or plateau that lies at the south-westerly end of Lake Chakmak, on the Little Pamir. It was first introduced to English knowledge by Major Montgomerie's Mirza in 1868-9, who, however, erroneously reported that it flowed out of the west end of Chakmak Lake. This stream, from its start to its junction with the main river, has a course of less than 10 miles, and is narrow, shallow, and quite without significance. It would be unworthy of mention in this context had not some travellers, such as M. Capus, regarded it as one of the parent streams, and had not the claim been also put forward to Lord Dunmore by some of the Russian officers whom he met. There is not a single argument in its favour. In the Russian map, the river or its valley figures, I know not why, as Kuntei-sai.

Third in order as we descend the main river, which below Bozai Gumbaz is variously called Wakhan-su, Wakhan-daria, Ab-i-Wakhan, and the Sarhad river, we come to the branch that flows in, also on the right bank, from the Great Pamir, where it rises in Wood's or

---

[1] Vide *Proceedings of the R.G.S.*, vol. xiv., January, 1892.

Victoria Lake. This is the river which was assumed by Wood, and by every one else in consequence of his discovery in 1838, to be the true parent stream of the Oxus, a mistake which, though natural enough on his part, it has taken fifty years to rectify, and which has given rise to at least one-half of the political confusion and diplomatic controversy arising out of the Boundary Agreement concluded by Lord Granville with Russia in 1872-3. The geographical basis of that agreement was the assumption that this branch was the head stream of the Oxus; and when it was found out not to be so, it is not surprising that great uncertainty and confusion should have ensued. This river is commonly marked on maps as the Pamir river, although the title Panja or Ab-i-Panj, which the main stream commonly bears below Kila Panja, is by some applied also to this upper branch. Neither in length, volume, nor any of the requisite characteristics, can it base any claim to be really accounted the parent stream, and we may therefore dismiss it from consideration.

It is not till a point some 160 miles below the confluence at Kala Panja, after the main river, now known indisputably as the Panja or Ab-i-panj, has made the great bend to the north at Ishkashim, after it has received from the east the united streams of the Shakh and Ghund Daras, after it has passed on its left bank Kala Bar Panja, the capital of Shighnan, and is approaching Kala Wamar, the capital of Roshan, on its right bank,—that there comes in from the east the only confluent that can attempt to seriously dispute the validity of the Panja's title. This is the river which, known above its confluence as Bartang (*i.e.* "narrow passage"), higher up as Murghab (*i.e.* "water-fowl"), and higher again as Aksu, originally emerges from the eastern end of Lake Chakmak on the Little Pamir, and throws a great loop round the middle Pamirs on the north, just as the Panja similarly encircles them on the south. The claim of the Murghab or Aksu to be the parent stream — first suggested some thirty years ago by the Russian geographer Veniukoff, and temporarily entertained, on political, perhaps, rather than on geographical grounds, by Sir H. Rawlinson and some other writers—has from time to time been revived, and has found favour with some who were unacquainted with the full geographical details. Although this hypothesis is not, I believe, now entertained by any one who can pretend to such knowledge, it may be well to state the reasons for which it cannot possibly be accepted.

The arguments which have been used in its support are as follows. Firstly, it has been suggested that the Greek name Oxus, by which the river in and above Bactria has been known since the days of Alexander, is a corruption of the Turkish name Ak-su (*i. e.* "white water") by which the Murghab is known in its upper course. Secondly, it has been stated that the entire length of the Aksu-Murghab-Bartang is greater than that of the Panja. And, thirdly, it has been suggested that it

c

receives a larger number of confluents in its passage. None of these contentions, however, can be established.

The theory that Oxus is merely a Greek transliteration of Aksu, is one of those purely fanciful identifications to which amateur etymology is particularly prone. In the first place, Aksu is the name only of a limited, and that the most insignificant, section of the Murghab or Bartang river, of whose existence it is scarcely possible that the Greeks can ever have been aware. When they came to Bactria, and asked the name of the great river, it is in the highest degree unlikely that the inhabitants would have given to them the name of a remote stream many hundred miles distant, of which not one of themselves had probably even so much as heard. Secondly, as a Turkish name, it is doubtful whether the name Aksu can have sprung into existence until long after the Hellenic form Oxus had been coined. Thirdly, that the name Oxus was the Greek transcription of some very early form appears to be certain. As to what this may have been authorities differ. Sir H. Rawlinson regarded it as the Hellenic version of Wakhsh, the name of the principal northern confluent of the great river, which, under the modern Persian title of Surkh-ab (identical with Kizil-su, or Red river), flows into it from the direction of the Alai, between Karategin and Darwaz, while he regarded the Persian form Wakhsh as identical with the Vakhshu of Sanskrit literature, which, in the Puranas, and in the traditions and travels of the early Buddhist pilgrims, is described as third of the four rivers of the Aryan paradise; and, with the Mongolian Bakhshu, the Tibetan Pakshu, and the Chinese Fotsu, all of them being names given to the same river—i. e. the Oxus—from very remote times. What may have been the original root of the Sanskrit Vakhshu is uncertain. *Vah* ("pure"), *vah* ("to flow"), and *vaksh* ("angry"), have been suggested. They may have been strengthened into it, or it may have been contracted into them.[1] With reference to his suggestion, I may observe that it appears to me unlikely that the Greeks would have named the main river from what was obviously only a tributary, even though a considerable tributary, in a part of its course with which they must have been perfectly familiar, and far above which they were thoroughly acquainted with the main stream.

Sir H. Yule sought the origin of the name in the same Sanskrit root, *veh* or *vah*, which he regarded as appearing in the various forms Wakh-an and Wakhsh, from the former of which he supposed the Ochus, mentioned as a Central Asian river in Strabo and Pliny, to have been derived, and from the later Oxus, Oxii, Oxiani.[2]

---

[1] *Vide* Sir H. Rawlinson's 'Monograph on the Oxus,' in the *Journal of the R.G.S.* vol. xlii., 1872, pp. 489, 496, 501.

[2] *Vide* Introduction to Wood's 'Oxus,' p. xxiii. He thinks, with plausibility, that the first of these forms reappears in the name Oech—undoubtedly the River Oxus—to which the Byzantine ambassadors from the Emperor Justinian to Dizabulus, Khan of the Turks, in 568 A.D., came on their return journey to Europe (*Ibid.*, p. xlii.).

Professor Vambéry, however, scouts these derivations, and says that Oxus was merely the Hellenized form of Oghuz or Okhuz, which was the old Turkish denomination of a big water or river. He cites the Sheibani-nameh, written at the end of the fifteenth century, where the Oxus is often called Oghuz, and he says that the Uz-boi or Turkoman name for the ancient bed of the same river existing in the desert south of Khiva, is a contraction of the same title. It seems to me, however, quite impossible that Turkish names should have prevailed in Bactria and Sogdiana at the time of Alexander, before the Turks had been so much as heard of; and it is noteworthy that in all the Mussulman chronicles and geographers, from the first appearance of the Arab conquerors in

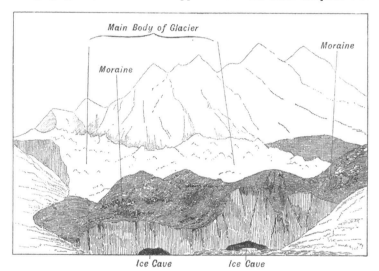

GLACIER SOURCE OF THE OXUS.

those regions, the name applied to the river is not Oxus, but Jaihun. If Oghuz was, and had been, its admitted title for centuries, why is it always designated by another?

To me it appears more likely that the Greeks of Alexander's day should have heard a Tajik or Iranian name, *i.e.* a word of Aryan descent; and whether this now unknown word was allied or not to the root-forms cited by Rawlinson and Yule, it may conceivably in its origin have sprung from that primordial form signifying water, which is variously supposed to reappear in the Latin *aqua*, French *Aix*, Erse *uisge*, Gaelic *usque*-baugh, English *whisky*, and in the river names Usk, Axe, Exe, Esk, Ox-ford, and Ouse.

The second argument in favour of the Aksu-Murghab is its

alleged superiority of length. The Russians say that from its source in the Chakmak Lake to Kala Wamar it is 252 miles in length; while the Panja from the glacier-source to the same point has been roughly estimated as 240 miles. I do not myself regard the test of mileage, particularly when the figures are so evenly balanced, as of any conclusive value. But I may say, from a double calculation of compass-reckoning, and ascertained length of marches, that I believe the course of the Panja to Kala Wamar to be not 240 but 270 miles, or nearly 20 miles in excess of the asserted length of the Aksu. So that even on the score of length the advantage is not, as claimed, to the Aksu, but to the Panja.

The third argument, viz. that the Aksu-Murghab receives a larger number of tributaries, can, of course, only mean that it contains a larger volume of water. Now, it is obvious that the sole method of applying this test is not by counting upon the fingers the respective number of confluents, but by measurement of the volume of the two streams at the point of junction. Not one of the advocates of the Aksu-Murghab theory, however, has ever visited Kala Wamar. On the other hand, Mr. Ney Elias, the only Englishman who has ever been there (in November, 1885), has recorded that from careful inspection and personal fording of both rivers, and from minute local inquiries as to their respective fluctuations, he was able to satisfy himself that the Panja is, at every season of the year but one, a very much more voluminous stream than the Murghab. That exception is in the summer months of June and July, when, owing to the much greater proximity of the main glacier feeders of the Murghab (viz. the Kashala Yakh at the head of the Kudara tributary, south-west of the Great Kara Kul) and to its more compressed channel and steeper bed (involving a greater fall per mile) between the Kudara junction and Kala Wamar, there is probably more water in the Murghab at the latter place than in the Panja; a view which was borne out by the native surveyor, despatched by Colonel Trotter, of the Forsyth Commission, to this spot in June, 1873. He reported that both the volume and velocity of the Murghab were greater at that season, but he made no attempt to ascertain their relative depth. As soon as this brief spate, due to the summer melting of the glacier surfaces, is over, the Murghab dwindles rapidly, and when Mr. Ney Elias saw it in the season of low water in 1885, it had somewhat less than half the volume of the Panja. He summed up by saying that of the three elements of which a river consists—breadth, velocity, and depth—the first is greater in the Murghab in summer and in the Panja in winter; the second is always greater in the Murghab; but the third, and most important, is always greater in the Panja; whilst, roughly speaking, the duration of winter to summer is as three to one.

I hope, therefore, I have shown incontestably that, upon each of the grounds put forward by the advocates of the Aksu-Murghab theory, their case breaks down. I may add that there are certain subsidiary criteria of the headwaters of a river, the application of which will be attended in each case with precisely the same result. If elevation of source be considered, then the Panja is easily the superior ; for whereas the height of Lake Chakmak was registered by Colonel Trotter as 13,200 feet, by Captain Younghusband as 13,850 feet, and by the Boundary Commission of 1895 as 13,100 feet, that of the glacier source of the Wakhjir was given by M. Dauvergne as 14,700 feet. If, on the other hand, total drainage area be taken into account, though, in the absence of more accurate surveys than we at present possess, I hesitate to dogmatize, yet a glance at the map will show that, to all appearances, the advantage is greatly on the side of the Panja.

There remain two other arguments, one based upon physical, the other upon historical grounds, which should not be without weight. To some extent the structure of a valley containing a river may be said to bear upon the question of its identity. That any one who had followed up the valley of the Panja to Kala Panja in the first place, or to Bozai Gumbaz in the second, and had at either of those places seen the main valley, with no physical interruption, continuing to pierce the mountains, should ever have entertained any doubt as to its containing the principal stream, seems to me very strange.[1]

The final argument is that of historical authority and popular acceptance. In the first place, it is noteworthy that, from as far back as records extend, the identity of the river below Kala Wamar with the

---

[1] And yet an almost unbroken succession of travellers and authorities, from Wood downwards, have been guilty of the error. Wood himself had serious qualms ; for when he came to the junction above Kala Panja, and had to make up his mind which branch to pursue—whether the Pamir confluent from Victoria Lake, or the Sirhad or Mastuj branch, as he called the Ab-i-Wakhan, from a mistaken idea that it somehow conducted into Mastuj and Chitral—he said, "To my eye the stream of Sirhad, as the river from Mastuch is frequently called, appeared the larger, but the Wakhanis held a different opinion." Had he followed his eye instead of his guides, the true source of the Oxus might have been determined half a century earlier, and the two governments of Great Britain and Russia might have been spared the long controversy over the ignorant agreement. Yule, following Wood, expressed some doubts as to whether the Pamir or the Sarhad were the real parent stream ; but writing as late as 1872, he entertained not the slightest suspicion of the existence of the real Wakhan source (which is not even indicated in his map to the new edition of Wood in that year), but accepted the account of Major Montgomerie's Mirza in 1869, who said that the Sarhad branch rose in the Little Pamir or Chakmak Lake. More remarkable is it, that even after the falsity of the latter hypothesis had been discovered, the subsequent travellers who came to Bozai Gumbaz, at the junction of the Sarhad and the Wakhjir stream, should have all but ignored the latter. Gordon in 1874, upon arriving at Bozai Gumbaz, merely remarked, "A stream from the eastern Taghdumbash Pamir joins here." Capus, in 1887, said nothing about it at all. Littledale, in 1890, said, "At Bozai Gumbaz another stream joined the Wakhan called Varjer" (i.e. Wakh-jir). Had any of these travellers, from Wood downwards, ever read the description of Macartney, which was written in 1809 and published in 1815, and which I shall quote presently, he could hardly have committed such an oversight.

Panja (and not with the Murghab) above has been assumed by the
inhabitants of the district, indicating that, in their opinion, this was
the parent stream. Like the Greek Oxus, so the Persian name Panja is
applied to the river both below and above Kala Wamar—in fact, over
the whole distance from Kala Panja to Kolab. Secondly, if we consult
the best-known Arab geographers—nay, even if we come down to the
present century, and study the writings of a countryman of our own—
we shall discover indications of the real truth so unmistakable that it
is surprising they should have been so completely overlooked. It is a
common consensus among the Arab writers that the Jaihun, as they
uniformly call it, rises in or near to Badakshan, a description which
can only refer to the southern or Wakhan branch, and not possibly to
the Murghab or Aksu. Istakhri, however, who wrote in the tenth
century, was even more precise. " The Jaihun rises under the name of
Jariab (or Khariab) in the land of Wakhan, which belongs to Badakshan. In Khotl and Wakhsh it receives several tributaries, which swell
it to a great river. The first of these is called Akhas or Halbak; the
next is the river Bartang; the third is the river Faraghi; the fourth is
the river Andijara ; the fifth is the Wakhshab, which is the greatest of all
these rivers.'' Edrisi, in the twelfth century, almost textually reproduced
this description, which, however we may identify the remaining four
confluents, at any rate expressly includes the Bartang or Murghab
among their number. Finally, if it be said that in none of these
accounts is the precise source indicated, but only the more southerly or
Panja branch, let me cite a memoir by Lieutenant Macartney, printed
as an appendix to Mountstuart Elphinstone's 'Kingdom of Caubul'
(published in 1815), in which, quoting from some native informant
whose name is not given, he supplies an almost absolutely correct
description of the Wakh-jir source, as I have already depicted it, and
concludes, with a prescience which for seventy years only one person was
found to imitate, and none to detect, that it was the true parent stream.
These are his words :

" The river Ammu, or Oxus, has its source from the high lands of Pamer. It
issues from a narrow valley 200 or 300 yards broad in Wakhan, the southern
boundary of Pamer. This valley is enclosed on three sides by the high snowy
mountain called Pooshtikhur [1] to the south, east, and west. The stream is seen
coming from under the ice, which is stated to be at least 40 spears in depth. The
spring itself could not be seen in consequence of the great mass of ice formed over
it ; but there can be no doubt of the spring's being on this hill under the ice, for
it does not appear that there was any opening or break in any of the three sides

---

[1] Pusht-i-Khur means literally, "Ass's Back," presumably from the shape of some
crest or summit of the mountain. Major Raverty (' Notes on Afghanistan,' p. 160)
thinks this is a fictitious title, which he supposes to have arisen from a confusion with
the Bushkar Darah, a valley on the western border of Chitral, over 150 miles away.
This is altogether unlikely. At the same time (p. 302) he accuses Macartney of having
confounded the glacier source of the Oxus with the glacier source of the Yarkhun or
Chitral river, whereas Macartney was quite right in distinguishing the sources of the
two rivers as rising on opposite sides of the central Hindu Kush watershed.

mentioned, by which it could come from a more distant place. I therefore conclude that this is the true head of the Oxus; at all events the greatest body of
water, though there are others which may have a more distant source. It is carried
north [1] in this narrow valley for 5 *coss*; [2] at 4 *coss* it is 20 yards broad, and breast
deep; and on leaving the valley, after having been joined by many other springs
from the same hill, it is 50 yards, and middle deep. The Shiber, or Adum Koosh,[3]
joins it 5 *coss* above Kilia Shah Jehan,[4] 25 *coss* below Pooshtikhur. In this distance
seven or eight streams, from knee to middle deep, and from 10 to 30 yards broad,
join it from the left bank." [5]

I submit that Lieutenant Macartney's native informant, whoever
he may have been, was a better-informed and a more competent
geographer than the host of big names who have succeeded him, and
I gladly disinter this forgotten passage, in order to lay a tardy wreath
upon its author's grave. I am the more ready to offer this compliment,
since the only competitor for its award, in the person of the single
follower to whom I have alluded, was also a native. Mohammed Amin
of Yarkand, the guide of the murdered Adolph Schlagintweit, supplied
to Pundit Manphul a geographical description of Chinese Turkestan and
the neighbouring regions, to the accuracy of which modern geographical
research lends ever-increasing testimony. In this report, which is printed
as an appendix to Davies' ' Report on the Trade Routes of the N.W.
Frontier,' in 1862, occurs a passage which I have never seen quoted, but
which, though fifty years later than Macartney, must share with him the
credit of perfectly faithful presentment. He says, " Another stream from
the Pamer Khurd lake (*i.e.* the Sarhad stream from Lake Chakmak)
falls into *the headwaters of the Daria-i-Panj* near Karwan balasi [6] (*i.e.* at
Bozai Gumbaz), *which have their source on the western side of the Kara-
chunkur pass* in the Pamer range (*i.e.* the Wakhjir Pass), below the
Piryakh peak in the Karakoram range." [7] The Piryakh peak is,
apparently, that which is elsewhere called Pirkhar,[8] and was described
by Macartney as Pusht-i-Khur. Had the scientific geographers who
made the careful Yarkandi's report the basis of speculations as ingenious
as they were mistaken, only paid attention to his written words, again

---

[1] The real direction is north-west.

[2] A *coss*, or *kos*, varies from 1 mile 4 furlongs to 1 mile 6 furlongs. It is the Hindu
equivalent of the *kuroh*, also a term of variable quantity, which prevails in Afghanistan.

[3] This is clearly the Sarhad, or Little Pamir confluent. The distance as given
is almost exactly correct.

[4] This must have been one of the forts whose ruins are still visible below Bozai
Gumbaz.

[5] This also is correct.

[6] Karwan or Caravan balasi is a name still applied to a piece of good grazing-
ground on the right bank of the Oxus, opposite to the junction of the Baikara stream.

[7] p. cccxxxiii.

[8] Pirkhar is a name now applied to the valley and stream that open out on the
left bank of the Oxus, immediately opposite to and south of Sarhad, and up which the
road goes to the Baroghil Pass. Piryakh or Piriokh, on the other hand, is the name of
a range of mountains on the 39th parallel between Karategin and Darwaz.

might the discovery of the true source of the Oxus have been anticipated by thirty years. It is fair also to mention that the Greek taveller,
Dr. Potagos, in 1870, though he did not visit the Wakhan source of the
Oxus, but diverged from it towards Lake Chakmak, was told by his
guides that the former was the real source of the Amu.[1]

It is worthy of mention, and was pointed out to me by the late
General J. T. Walker, that the source of the Oxus, thus described, does
not spring from the higher range of the Hindu Kush. It is a well-
known fact that most of the principal rivers of the Himalayas do not
rise in those ranges, but in the country behind them to the north, afterwards breaking through them on their way to the south. Thus their
sources are really several thousand feet lower than the sources of the
smaller rivers which rise in the southern fall of the Himalayas. The
same phenomenon also occurs in the Hindu Kush. The Hunza river
rises considerably to the north of the anial range of the Hindu Kush,
and breaks through on its way to the south. Thus the water-parting
is thrown considerably to the north, and is very much lower than the
anial range. It is on the reverse side of this water-parting that the
Oxus has its source.

To revert to my journey. Having marched down the Wakhan
Pamir to Bozai Gumbaz [2]—where Captain Younghusband, after being
visited in a friendly way by the Russians, and after having entertained
them, was arrested by Colonel Yonoff in August, 1891, on the return
of the latter from his excursion across the Indian frontier—I diverged
to the north-east to visit the Chakmak Lake and the Little Pamir. In
the valley between the lake and Bozai Gumbaz, which is half a mile wide
at the bottom, and about 12 miles in length, the Sarhad branch of the
Oxus meanders about with a very tortuous course in a bed 20 yards
wide, through scenery that very fairly recalls that of a swampy Scotch
moor. There is, however, a great deal of sand and stones and clay, and
the ground sparkles with immense patches of saline efflorescence.
The Sarhad branch is recruited by three or four streams which come
down from gorges in the mountains on the north side of the valley, but
which, at the time of my visit, were almost empty rills. As we ascend

---

[1] 'Dix Années de Voyage dans l'Asie Centrale' (Paris, 1885), vol. i. p. 70. Dr.
Potagos, however, owing to a confusion between the Great and Little Pamirs, and to
his ignorance of the existence of the former, is entirely at sea in his criticism of previous
travellers, notably of Marco Polo and Wood.

[2] Bozai Gumbaz, or the Tomb of Bozai, sometimes also and more strictly called
Gumbaz-i-Bozai, is a conical mud cupola resting upon a square brick foundation, at a
little distance above the confluence of the Sarhad and Wakhan streams. The Russians,
in 1891, tried to set up a claim to its possession, on the ground that Boza or Bozai had
been a Kokandian tax-gatherer, who was killed down there while in the service of his
state. Investigation proved this story to be a myth, and Bozai to have been a small
local chieftain, who was slain in a fight with the Kanjutis or Hunza freebooters fifty
years ago. The elevation was determined by the Boundary Commission of 1895 as
12,880 feet.

the valley, the ground becomes broken up into clay hills, and presently we reach a sort of low plateau several feet higher than the river-bed, stretching for nearly 4 miles to the lake. It is bare and flattish on the top, and contains a small lake between 300 and 400 yards long, as well as several largish pools. This is the watershed between the Chakmak Lake, with its easterly drainage into the Aksu basin, and the westerly drainage of the Panja or Oxus valley. In the Russian map this low plateau is called the Andemania Pass.[1] It is not a pass at all, but a miniature plateau. There is no Andemania or Andemin Pass here, and the latter name has been correctly transferred on English maps—*e.g.* Mr. Littledale's R.G.S. map—to the Benderski Pass between the Little and Great Pamirs, on the further side of the Chakmak Lake, of which it is the native title.

Reaching the edge of the lake, whose waters glinted brightly in the sun, I followed its northern shore over ground that was alternately soft grass, spongy bog, and dry stones, towards the north-east extremity. There I found to my surprise that the main body of the lake, which is from 3½ to 4 miles in length, has an extension in its extreme easterly corner, of which I have found no notice in previous descriptions. Through a channel a few hundred yards wide, the water spreads into a succession of bays or extensions, each of which looks like a separate lake, and which are relieved by promontories and islets. These protract the length of the lake proper for an additional 1½ to 2 miles. It is from the extremity of the easternmost of these bays that the Aksu river emerges, flowing in two or three channels with a slow current through a rushy bed about 30 to 40 yards wide. This is the source of the rival claimant to the parentage of the Oxus, of whose pretensions I have already disposed. From here the Aksu wanders down the Little Pamir, spreading out into marshy swamps and ill-defined lakelets, which on most maps appear as though they were a series of accurately determined lakes. On the other hand, there are two biggish sheets of water in the hills immediately above the easterly extension of the lake or archipelago which appear in no map, and which have no connection with the river or its swamps. From the source of the Aksu, the Little Pamir stretches away with an average breadth of from 2 to 3 miles in the direction of Aktash, a normal Pamir landscape, closed by a snowy mountain at the end of the vista. A domed Kirghiz *ziarat* stood out clearly to the north-east, but on no part of this Pamir did I observe any sign of habitation or of human life.

As regards the name of the lake, I have called it Chakmak, because that appeared to be the generally accepted local designation.[2] In some

---

[1] Grombchevski in 1888 called it the Chilob (*i.e.* Chelap) or Andemanyn Pass.

[2] The first mention that I have found of the name is in one of the routes by Mohammed Amin, in 1867. He calls it Chakmaklig. *Vide* Davies' 'Report on Trade Routes,' Appendix iv. B.

maps it has been written Chakmaktin. Gordon and Trotter called it Gaz or Oi Kul, *i.e.* in Turki " Goose Lake," which is a common title applied by the Kirghiz to any or all of the Pamir lakes. Regel, the Russian, is quite alone in applying the name Suman Kul. The Russian map names the series of swamps or lakelets further down the valley successively as Turdûnin Kul and Karadumer Kul. Lake Chakmak possesses yet additional names, for whereas English writers have frequently employed the title Little Pamir Lake, which is the Kul-i-Pamir-Khurd of the Wakhis, the natives have also described it to travellers as Durna Kul or Tourna Kul (which I suspect to be the same word as the Russian title just quoted), and as Barkat Yasin (explained by Gordon as meaning

BOZAI GUMBAZ.

Burgut Nursi, *i.e.* the " Eagle's Place or Nest "). I believe myself that the last-named is the name rather of one of the neighbouring ravines ; and the same applies to the name Chelap, which was also given to me, and has appeared in some maps as appertaining to the lake, but which seems to belong preferably to the district in which it is situated. Colonel Trotter gave the elevation of the lake as 13,200 feet ; Captain Younghusband as 13,850 feet ; Lord Dunmore's aneroid, which appears to have been uniformly as treacherous as was my own, made it 14,230 feet. The Boundary Commission of 1895 made the source of the Aksu 13,100 feet. The Mirza's figures in 1869, 13,300 feet, were therefore wonderfully near the mark.

Pursuing the discussion of the hydrography of the Pamirs, I pass from this point to the next or Great Pamir, in order to make clear its lake-system. The central feature is, of course, Wood's or Victoria Lake, from the western extremity of which the Panja flows. When Wood arrived at this lake in midwinter (February 19, 1838), land and water were equally covered with snow, and were almost indistinguishable from each other. He accordingly accepted the Kirghiz measurements of length and breadth, 14 miles by an average of 1 mile, checked so far as possible by his own vision. When Gordon and Trotter were there in April, 1874, the lake was similarly frozen over and snow-covered; but they estimated its dimensions as 10 miles by 3. Littledale, in June, 1890, found the lake still half sheeted with the previous winter's ice, but was much struck with its narrowness, which reminded him of a canal. Lord Dunmore, in November, 1892, gave its length as 9 to 10 miles in winter, and 12 miles in summer. The explanation of these varying figures is that, in common with all the Pamir lakes, Victoria Lake varies in size according to the season of the year, the normal dimensions being about 10 miles by 1½ mile, which are enlarged by the annual inundation of a larger area, consequent upon the melting of the summer snows. M. Benderski, however, the Russian topographer, who first saw the lake in 1883, and was attached to the Pamir Boundary Commission in 1895, told the English members of the latter that the lake had greatly diminished in size in the interval, and that he expected it finally to disappear. If the same process has been going on for centuries, we may perhaps find herein an explanation of the apparently extravagant dimensions assigned to the lake (assuming it to be identical with the Dragon Lake of legend) by the Chinese Buddhist pilgrims. As regards its elevation, Wood (whose instrument must have been defective) registered the height by boiling-point at 15,600 feet. Later measurements (Trotter, 13,900 feet; Littledale, 13,980 feet; Boundary Commission, 1895, 13,390 feet) have familiarized us with more modest figures. Touching the name of this lake, the title Victoria Lake, suggested rather than given to it by Wood, whose discovery coincided with the year following upon Her Majesty's accession, seems on the whole to have won most favour, at least with Englishmen. The alternative name of Sir-i-kol, which was mentioned to Wood by the Kara Kirghiz, has been very plausibly explained as referring to the station or camp at the "Head of the Lake;" although some have preferred Sarik or Sarigh-Kol, i.e. Yellow Lake. In the Anglo-Russian Pamir Agreement of March, 1895, the Russian name for the lake is given as Zor Kul. Faiz Bakhsh, the surveyor who was despatched to the Pamirs in 1870 by Sir D. Forsyth during the first Yarkand expedition, called the lake Hauz Kalan, i e. Great Pool, or Kol-i-Sikandari, Alexander's Lake—a name which has been mentioned by no other traveller.[1] The former title is identical with the Kul-i-Kalan of Trotter and Gordon, which may either

---

[1] *Journal of the R.G.S.*, vol. xlii., 1872, p. 465.

signify literally the Great Lake, or be a contraction of the longer form Kul-i-Pamir-i-Kalan, *i.e.* Great Pamir Lake. The name Gaz Kul (Goose Lake) was given to Littledale as the common Kirghiz title; but I have already explained that this is a generic designation applied equally by the natives to any of the Pamir lakes.

A feature already noticed in the valley of the Chakmak Lake also holds good of the Victoria Lake basin, viz. the presence of a chain of smaller lakes in the immediate neighbourhood of and in connection with the main sheet of water. Two such small and frozen lakes were first observed by Gordon and Trotter in 1874, at a slight distance from the

LITTLE PAMIR AND AKSU RIVER.

upper or eastern end of Victoria Lake. Littledale calls one of these lakes, which is "some miles to the east" of the big lake, Aidin Kul. Lord Dunmore applies to one of the number the now familiar designation of Gaz Kul. The Russian map calls the more westerly of the two Lake Kurkuntai, a name which reappears on the Indian Intelligence map as Kuruntea. A further small sheet of water to the east, from which rises the Istik drainage, is called Lake Karadungi. At the eastern extremity of these lakelets is the watershed separating the Panja and Aksu drainages; and here the river Istik or Issik (erroneously called Isligh in Gordon's book) rises from several sources, and flows towards the Aksu, whence it joins at some distance below Aktash. The channel of one of the streams that flows from the watershed on the south into the eastern end of Victoria Lake also spreads out into three small lakes at the bottom of the valley as it approaches the main sheet of water.

Similar conditions, on a larger scale, may be predicated of the hydrography of the next or Alichur Pamir. Here the lie of the lakes and the direction of the main drainage is again from east to west. The principal body of water is the Yeshil Kul (Green Lake), or Ishal Kul of Pundit Manphul and Isil-kol of Chinese records. This is the finest expanse of water in the Pamirs, being little liable to contraction, owing to its greater depth and more precipitous banks. It possesses a length of from 16 to 20 miles, and a breadth that varies, owing to the peculiar indentations of the shore, from 1 mile to 3 miles, and its elevation is 12,550 feet. From its western extremity issues the Ghund or Gunt river, which, after its junction with the Shakh Dara confluent of the Oxus lower down, flows for a few miles under the title Suchan Dara, and disembogues into the main stream of the Panja, a little above Kala Bar Panja, the capital of Shighnan.

A promontory projecting into Yeshil Kul at its eastern end has been the scene of a twofold historical tragedy, the earlier of which events is said to have been the origin of its name. In 1759, when the Chinese took possession of Kashgar, the two Kalmuk Khojas whom they expelled fled in a westerly direction across the Pamirs towards Badakshan. The Chinese general Fouteb, *i.e.* Fu or Ku Ta-jen, pursuing them by forced marches, came up with the fugitives at the east end of Yeshil Kul, attacked them by night, and inflicted upon them a defeat, from which, however, the Khojas and the bulk of their followers escaped with their lives.[1] Gordon was told in the Pamirs that they drove several of their women and children, mounted on camels and horses, into the lake, in order to avoid by drowning the worse fate that they anticipated at the enemy's hands, and that ever since sounds of lamentation have been heard to rise from the waters.[2] The Chinese general inscribed upon a stone a trilingual record in Chinese, Manchu, and Turki of his exploit, which remained there until recent years, when the Russians transported as much of it as remained to their museum at Tashkend. The place was thenceforward known as Soma Tash, which is explained as meaning Written Stone.[3]

---

[1] *Vide* the interesting letter from two Jesuit priests at Kashgar dated November 26, 1759, and published in *Lettres Edifiantes*, xxxi. 248.

[2] 'Roof of the World,' p. 158.

[3] Lord Dunmore in his first map spelled it *Somur*. But in his book (vol. ii. p. 167) he substitutes for this *Surma*, which he says means "black." Now, *Surma* is a Persian word, signifying not "black," but "antimony" or "collyrium," the material used by the Persians for darkening the eyebrows and eyelids. A Persian word may conceivably have been joined with the Turki word *tash*, "stone," but the particular combination is more absurd than would be Rouge-hill for Redhill, in Surrey. I made many inquiries on the subject, but with no satisfactory results. The Kirghiz head-man of the Taghdumbash said the name was not Surma, but Suma Tash, and signified "written stone." On the other hand, the Hunza Wazir thought it was a word meaning "marsh-land" (cf. *su* = in Turki, "water").

The second incident of bloodshed with which the promontory of Soma Tash has been connected, happened less than three years ago. The Alichur Pamir and Yeshil Kul in particular had been for many years the more or less disputed boundary-line between the Afghan and Chinese spheres of jurisdiction on the Pamirs, when, in the early summer of 1891, Colonel Yonoff was despatched by the Russian Government with a body of troops, facetiously christened the Hunting Detachment, nominally in order to shoot *Ovis Poli*, and to indulge in rifle-practice on the Pamirs (of all places in the world!); really to execute a demonstration over the entire region, to turn out any Chinese or Afghan soldiers who might be found, and to anticipate the proposed diplomatic settlement of the dispute with England by forcible annexation. The Chinese, hearing of this movement, sent an officer with a small body of troops to assert their claims at Soma Tash. A gallant young English officer, Lieutenant Davison, who was travelling on his own responsibility in Chinese Turkestan at the time, and had been commissioned by Captain Younghusband from Kashgar to report upon what was passing in the Pamirs, was on the Alichur at the same juncture. Colonel Yonoff, arriving at Soma Tash, ordered the Chinese *Yangdarin* to withdraw, which command the latter with characteristic promptitude obeyed. Simultaneously he arrested Lieutenant Davison and sent him back, *viá* the Alai and Marghilan, to Kashgar, an unwarrantable proceeding for which the Russian Government subsequently apologized. The Russians having in the mean time withdrawn, the Chinese again turned up at Soma Tash, and proceeded to build a fort. In the spring of 1892, however, the Afghans, who also claimed Soma Tash, appeared upon the scene, and the Chinese with docile rapidity a second time retired. Colonel Yonoff, however, was not to be foiled. In the summer of 1892 he repeated his military promenade of the previous year; ordered the Chinese to evacuate their armed posts on Lake Rang Kul and at Aktash (on the Aksu), which, of course, they did without a murmur; and, arriving at Soma Tash, essayed the same tactics with the Afghan outpost whom he found there installed. The Afghan commander, though hopelessly outnumbered, refused, and a conflict ensued on June 22, 1892, in which fifteen out of the seventeen Afghans present were slain. The Russians then again withdrew.

Just as in the cases of Lakes Chakmak and Victoria, so here at the eastern extremity of Yeshil Kul is a small subsidiary lake-basin, in the valley of the Alichur river, which contains no fewer than five lakes, scarcely as yet indicated on any map. They lie among the hollows and between " a sea of gravel mounds," the moraine-deposits of ancient glaciers. The nearest of these to Yeshil Kul is Bulun Kul,[1] which

---

[1] This must not be confounded with a second Bulun Kul, a lake which lies on the western side of the Gez defile, on the main line of connection between Kashgar and the northern Pamirs.

LITTLE PAMIR, NEAR MIHMAN-GULI PASS.

lies to the south of its eastern termination, and is connected with it by a stream only half a mile in length. Separated by a low watershed from this lake is another Gaz Kul, or Goose Lake. Next to this is Khargosh Kul, or Hare's Lake, so called because it lies below the Khargosh Dawan, or Hare's Pass, leading to the Great Pamir. This little lake is named Chukur Kul on the Russian Intelligence Map. The fourth in order to the east is Tuz Kul, or Salt Lake; and the fifth and last is Sassigh, or Sasik Kul [1] (*i.e.* Stinking or Fetid Lake), which is about 8 miles long by 1 broad.[2] Eastwards from this point the Alichur valley continues for a distance of 3 miles to Chatir, or Chadir Tash (Tent Rock), a solitary rock standing up in the valley-bottom, and presenting, at a distance, the appearance of a tent.

The next Pamir lake-system to which, in our northerly progress, we come, is that of Rang Kul, lying in the hollow of the Pamir that bears the same name. This has been explained by Yule and others ,as signifying Ibex Lake (*rang* being the Turki word for the wild goat). Mr. Ney Elias, however, reported that the peoples of those regions use the word *taka* in preference for ibex (*cf.* the Min-taka pass before mentioned), and accordingly he preferred the Persian interpretation of *rang*, i.e. variegated, or of many colours.[3] I agree with this derivation, on the further ground that it is from their colour that several of the neighbouring lakes (*cf.* Kara Kul, or Black Lake; Yeshil Kul, or Green Lake; and possibly Sarik Kul, or Yellow Lake) are named. On the other hand, I have read that the Russians derive the name from a coarse sedge. Rang Kul was reported by Pundit Manphul, upon the information of Mohammed Amin, as lying in the Pamir Khurd, or Little Pamir [4]—a deception that greatly puzzled Yule and other geographers. As a matter of fact, it is situated in a north-east bay or extension of the valley of the Ak-baital (White Mare), which is the

---

[1] Colonel Yule, misled by the exaggerated dimensions given to these small lakes in earlier native itineraries or in Chinese geographies, and by the imperfect information existing in his time, went quite wrong over their identification. He thought, with Major Montgomerie, that Sasik Kul was Victoria Lake; that Pulong (*i.e.* Bulun) Kul was the imaginary Rang Kul of the Little Pamir; and that Tuz Kul was, possibly, Victoria Lake also (Introduction to Wood's 'Oxus,' pp. lxxxvi., lxxxvii.). Almost all the theoretical geographers, even the most distinguished, have been deceived by the fantastic exaggerations as to distance and measurement to which Oriental travellers invariably succumb.

[2] Abdul Mejid, in his northward march across the Pamirs to Kokand in 1861, mentions having passed two lakes, " at Khurgoshee and Kurreh Kol." The former he identifies in his itinerary with Sussugh Kul; the latter is the Great Kara Kul. His next march, after Kurreh Kol, is described as 15 miles in length, and as terminating at Dysame lake; but there can be little doubt that this is a misprint for the same lake, alluding to his day's march along its eastern shore.

[3] *Cf.* the well-known Karun river in south-west Persia, which is more strictly Kuran, or Kuh-rang, and is so called from the " variegated mountain " in which it takes its rise.

[4] *Vide* Appendix to Davies' 'Report on Trade Routes,' p. cccxxxiii.

northerly confluent—commonly dry in winter—of the Aksu, after its junction with which the latter river, flowing westwards, is called Murghab. Only in this remote sense—the Ak-baital valley being a physical continuation of the Aksu valley, and the Aksu valley being a physical continuation of the Little Pamir—can the Rang Kul lake be said to have any connection with the Pamir-i-Khurd, from which it is really severed by a great distance. Its elevation is 12,250 feet above the sea.

This lake, however, like those already discussed, occupies a lacustrine basin, the sheets of water in which vary in size and configuration according to the season of the year. Severtsoff described it as consisting in reality of three separate basins and an extensive marsh, connected by narrow straits. The main lake has two divisions—Shor Kul on the west and Rang Kul on the east, which are usually so united. In the high waters of summer the two form one unbroken sheet. Lord Dunmore, passing on November 20, 1892, at the opposite extreme of season, found them entirely severed by a neck of land a quarter of a mile across, and unconnected, and erroneously declined to believe that they were ever united. In winter-time the upper or eastern lake, thus diminished, resembles a series of swamps, dotted with islands, whose banks are incrusted with a saline efflorescence. The entire lake-basin is about 20 miles long, and the normal length of the lakes is—Rang Kul 4 miles, and Shor Kul 6 miles. A remarkable feature of these lakes is that neither does any river discharge into them, nor is there any river-exit. Their waters must accordingly be largely recruited by subterranean drainage from the hills. Mr. Ney Elias, in 1885, said that the upper lake was considered to be fresh and the lower salt. Captain Younghusband, in 1890, reported the water as salt, and the colour as a beautiful clear blue. On the southern shore of Shor Kul is a peculiar rock, with a sheer front of 100 feet, which is known as Chiragh Tash or Lamp Rock, from a peculiar illusion produced by the sun's light penetrating through a cave or orifice that is pierced right through the rock. The natives attribute it to the eye of a dragon who is supposed to lurk in the cave. Captain Younghusband, in 1890, was the first to dissipate the mystery by clambering up and discovering the illusion which had puzzled Ney Elias in 1885.[1] At a little distance from the eastern extremity of Rang Kul is the fort which the Russians have built and garrisoned, since they expelled the Chinese from Rang Kul (which lay far inside the Chinese frontier) in 1892.

There remains but one more lake in the Pamir area, viz. the Great Kara Kul, which lies in the Khargosh or Hare Pamir, on the northern edge of the Pamir region, below the great Trans-Alai range. This is the most considerable body of water in the district, and has by some been identified with the Dragon Lake of local, and still more of Chinese legend. Its dimensions have been absurdly exaggerated in the itineraries

---

[1] *Proceedings of the R.G.S.*, vol. xiv., 1892, p. 227.

of mediæval pilgrims. Its extreme length from north to south is in
reality 14¼ miles, its breadth from east to west 11 miles, and its elevation above the sea is 12,800 feet. Like Rang Kul, it consists of two
sheets of water united by a narrowish strait in the centre; or, as one
may otherwise put it, of a single lake very nearly cut in twain by two
promontories or sandy ridges projecting from the north and south shores.
The curious thing about this lake is, that legend with singular unanimity
has insisted at very varying periods upon a river discharge from it
towards the west or south. At one time this discharge was supposed to
be connected with the Surkhab or river of Karategin, at another with the
Murghab or Bartang, at a third with the Aksu. And yet while several
small torrents pour their waters into the lake, and one rather larger
stream, the Chon-su, joins it from the Tuyuk or Ak-baital Pass on the
south, there is no present efflux at all. The explanation appears to be,
as Kostenko, its first European explorer in 1876, remarked, that the lake-
level was once much higher than it is now, and that in those days it
may have had a double discharge, both to the north and to the south.
Severtsoff, indeed, said that even now, with a strong northerly wind
blowing, the water of the lake will sometimes in flood-time be driven
up the channel of the Chon-su, and then break out westwards in the
direction of the Murghab; but this appears to be a very rare phenomenon, and the absence of modern outlet must be accepted as an established
fact. The mountains approach closely to the lake and even project into
it on its western side; at its eastern end they are nearly 7 miles
distant, and hence the track from the north usually skirts that shore.
The strongly indented coasts are carved into frequent promontories,
and there is one island nearly 5 miles long. In stormy weather Kara
Kul presents a splendid spectacle, for its waters toss and boil like a
seething cauldron. Littledale, Younghusband, and Cumberland are the
only Englishmen who have seen it.[1]
   Though lying in a different basin, and outside the Pamirs proper, I
should, perhaps, not omit to notice the Little Kara Kul and its small
lacustrine satellites, less for its own sake than on account of the two
great mountain peaks which, at a distance of some 20 miles from each
other, soar into the air on the north-east and the south-east borders of
the lake, and which have given rise to much confusion among travellers
and geographers. One of these peaks is visible from the plain of
Yarkand and from Kashgar, whence it was roughly fixed, in 1868, by
Hayward, and more accurately, in 1874, by Colonel Trotter, who gave its
height as 25,350 feet. Both called it Tagharma, because the people said
it was near to the place and plain of that name.[2] A little later, when

   [1] *Vide* Kostenko's account of it in *Journal of the R.G.S.*, vol. xlvii., 1877, p. 29.
   [2] *Taghar* is a Turki word signifying "a bag of grain"—an allusion to the fertility
of the surrounding valley.

Trotter was in Sarikol, he saw from the southern side a different peak which was also called the Tagharma Peak. In 1876 Kostenko, from the Uzbel Pass, observed a great peak in this direction, the name of which was given to him as Mustagh Ata, *i.e.* Father of Ice Mountains. Maps and descriptions continued to confuse these separate mountains, usually representing them as one, until, in 1885, Mr. Ney Elias proved conclusively by his angles that they were distinct. The one to the northeast of Little Kara Kul is the mountain seen from Kashgar (from which it obscures the other), but is erroneously called Tagharma. He gave it the name Mount Dufferin, which appears in the Indian maps, but which, in a region lying so far outside of British-Indian influence, cannot, I think, be pressed. The Russian map calls it Mount Charkum, but I believe the real name has since been determined as Kungur. The second and southerly peak (which from Sarikol obscures the first) is the real Mustagh Ata, the height of which is probably a little less than its nameless brother, being calculated at about 25,000 feet, but which is a far finer mountain, since it is conical and comparatively isolated, whereas the more northerly mountain is the highest crest of an extended ridge. Even now the maps unanimously err in assigning to Mustagh Ata the altitude which appertains to its rival.

Several Russian explorers, notably Bogdanovitch in 1879 and Ivanoff in 1883, have made careful examination of Mustagh Ata, and during 1894, Dr. Sven Hedin, the Swedish traveller and scientist, made four unsuccessful attempts to climb it, reaching on one occasion to a height of 19,500 feet.[1] The summit, which is the central peak of three, is therefore still virgin, and is regarded by Hedin as almost inaccessible. The sides of this magnificent mountain are rent by deep gorges and filled with enormous glaciers.

Little Kara Kul, lying between them at a distance of about 50 miles due east from Rang Kul, has been formed by the moraines of a retreated glacier, which have dammed the valley. Glacier waters replenish it from the south, but its sole outlet is on the north into the upper course of the Gez stream, which flows towards Kashgar. A little below the point of discharge this stream receives from the north-west the drainage of a small chain of lakes in a separate basin, the lowest of which is called Basik Kul. Further down the Gez valley is the second Bulun Kul, which has already been mentioned.

From a description of the lake-system of the various Pamirs, I now turn to an account of the passes by which they are connected, and which I will trace in the inverse direction from north to south. I hope to have now sufficiently demonstrated that the Pamir region, in contradistinction to long-accepted beliefs, but in remarkable accordance with a prediction of Mr. Shaw,[2] consists of a series of elevated mountain valleys whose

---

[1] Vide *Geographical Journal*, vol. v., 1895, p. 154; and vol. vi. p. 350.
[2] *Vide* Yule's Introduction to Wood's ' Oxus,' p. lxxxix.

uniform direction is from east to west (with an occasional inclination from north-east to south-west),[1] which contract into gorges at their western extremities, where they become merged in the mountain systems of Roshan, Shighnan, and Wakhan; which are separated from each other by lofty parallel ridges whose normal trend is from east to west, directing the drainage into the Oxus basin; and which on the eastern side are fenced in and divided from the rival basin of Kashgar by a meridional range or ranges, sometimes included, in the mediæval itineraries and in the geographies based upon them, among the Tsung Ling, sometimes confounded with the obscure Bolor mountains,

CAMP SCENE, PAMIRS.

and throwing up at one point the mighty pinnacles of Mustagh Ata, and its twin peak. To pass, therefore, from one Pamir to another by the shortest route, it is necessary to follow the transverse gorges or to climb the lower saddles of the intervening ridges. Of these passes there are many, even if we do not accept Ivanoff's interpretation of the native adage, " There are no roads on the Pamirs," as signifying that the Pamirs are everywhere traversable, which they certainly are not. I propose to indicate the principal and most easily accessible of these lines of communication.

---

[1] I except from this summary the Taghdumbash Pamir, which, I have previously shown, lies outside of the Pamirs proper, and is part of a different basin.

I. Passes on to the Northern Pamirs.

Upon the north, the base of any advance upon the Pamirs from the Russian province of Ferghana is either Osh or Marghilan. The former is the route almost invariably adopted both by military forces and by travellers. From Osh the route proceeds to Gulcha, and thence across the Little Alai range by the Taldik Pass (Littledale, 11,600 feet; Russian and Indian maps, 12,070 feet), or by the adjoining passes of Archat-dawan (11,900 feet) or Shart (12,800 feet), on to the Alai Plateau, or upper valley of the Surkhab or Kizil-su. Striking across this valley, we approach the Great or Trans-Alai range, and, crossing it by the Kizil-art Pass (14,260 feet), descend upon the Great Kara Kul (12,800 feet). The route skirts the east shore of the lake, and then takes one of two directions : either (1) a more easterly course, followed by M. Bonvalot's party in 1887, viâ the Karazak Pass, and Uzbel or Kizil-jik Pass (Indian map, 15,190 feet; Russian map, 15,300 feet), on to the Rang Kul Pamir and lake, and thence to the junction of the Ak-baital and Aksu at Murghabi ; or (2) a more southerly course, taken by Littledale in 1890, up the Mus-kol or Chon-su confluent of Kara Kul to the Tuyuk or Ak-baital Pass (Russian map, 15,070 feet; Littledale, 15,525 feet), and thence down the Ak-baital stream to Murghabi, and the upper end of the Sarez Pamir.

The more westerly route to the northern Pamirs from Marghilan takes the following line : Uch Kurghan ; up the Isfairam river ; over the Little Alai range by the Tengiz Pass (11,800 feet) to Daraut Kurghan on the Kizil-su in the Alai Plateau ; across the Great or Trans-Alai range by the Ters-agar or Altindi Pass (12,000 feet) to Altin Mazar ; thence by the Takhta-koram Pass (15,480 feet) or Yengi Dawan (15,300 feet) on to the upper waters of the Kudara river, which can be followed down to their junction with the Murghab, or from which a shorter track can be taken more to the east over the Kara-bulak Pass (14,460 feet) to Kara-bulak on the Murghab.

II. Passes from the Murghab Valley and Sarez Pamir on to the Alichur Pamir and Yeshil Kul.

1. Starting from the Russian fort of Murghabi or Pamirski Poste, at the junction of the Aksu and Ak-baital streams, the route commonly followed ascends the Kara-su confluent of the Murghab, and crosses the low and flat-topped Neza Tash (i.e. Spear-stone) Pass (Indian map, 13,650 feet; Littledale, 14,200 feet) to the headwaters of the Alichur river, which is then followed eastwards, past Chatir Tash to Yeshil Kul.

2. A little to the west of this route is a tract that was followed from Murghabi by Putiata in 1883. It crosses the dividing range by the Buz-tere Pass (14,900 feet), and also debouches on the upper waters of the Alichur river.

3. Immediately to the west of this again is a pass called Agal-khar.

4. From this point the northern boundary range of the Alichur Valley and Pamir is not again pierced by a traversable route until we come to the Marchenai Pass (15,700 feet), leading down from Sarez on the Murghab to the northern shore of Yeshil Kul.

5. To the west of this, the Lenger Pass conducts through the same range to the western extremity of the lake.

III. PASSES FROM THE ALICHUR PAMIR AND THE GREAT PAMIR.

1. Beginning on the east in the mountain cluster that separates the drainage of the Aksu from that of the Alichur, we find a route that

FORT OF TASHKURGHAN.

leaves the Aksu river at some distance above Murghabi, ascends the Shor-bulak confluent to the pass of that name (14,700 feet), and then, crossing the Sari-tash Pass, comes down upon the valley of the Istik river, which can then be ascended in a south-west direction towards the watershed that divides its headwaters from those of Victoria Lake.

2. At some distance to the west a track leads from Chatir Tash up the Gorumdi confluent of the Alichur river, and crosses the Teter-su or Tetez Pass to the headwaters of the Istik.

3. In the same mountain range separating the Alichur drainage from the Victoria Lake basin on the south-west, and from the Istik or Aksu drainage on the south-east, there is at no great distance a pass named Kojiguit, which was crossed by Littledale and Dunmore.

4. Continuing westwards, we find a pass named Kara Bilis ("Black Pass"), which was first crossed by Ivanoff in 1883, but which supplies a collateral rather than a direct communication between the Alichur and Great Pamirs.

5. The next pass encountered is the lofty and very difficult one of Bash Gumbaz (16,460 feet), crossing the main range between the Alichur river (which is left at Abdullah Khan below Chatir Tash) and the western end of Victoria Lake. Ivanoff explored it in 1883. Littledale found it blocked by snow in June, 1890.

6. The next route conducts from Sasik Kul southwards over a pass which was named by Dunmore Hauz Dawan, from a small lake on its summit, but which appears on the Russian map as Kumdi (elsewhere Kundey). The route comes out upon the Pamir river a little below Victoria Lake.

7. The easiest of the passes between the small lake-basin above Yeshil Kul and the Great Pamir is, however, the next in order, viz. the Khargosh, or Hare Pass (14,450 feet), which debouches upon the Ab-i-Khargosh confluent of the Pamir river.

8. A little further to the west, a track leads from Bulun Kul, over the Koh-i-Tezek Pass (14,200 feet) and Kok-bai Pass (14,400 feet), on to the Mas confluent of the Pamir river, which it reaches at a point named Jangalik or Yumkhana, below Yol Mazar. These passes were explored by Putiata in 1883.

9. It is by following the same stream, the Mas, that communication is also effected between the valley of the Pamir river and the head-waters of the Shakh-dara river (which flows into the Ghund a little above its junction with the Oxus opposite Kala Bar Panja) over a pass, closed by snow except in summer, which Trotter called the Joshangaz, but which appears on most maps as the Mas Pass (15,120 feet).

IV. PASSES FROM THE GREAT PAMIR TO THE LITTLE PAMIR.

1. Gordon and Trotter, returning in 1874 from the Great Pamir and Victoria Lake to the Aksu valley below Aktash, followed down the Istik river, before mentioned.

2. If, however, access is sought to the same valley above Aktash, *i.e.* to the Little Pamir proper, the upper course of the Istik known as the Chish-tiube can be ascended, and the bordering range of the Little Pamir be crossed by either the Kizil Rabat Pass or the Urta Bel Pass (14,090 feet), which lead down on to the string of lakes below Chakmak Kul. The watershed between the two drainages, in the case of the latter pass, is at a very short distance above the valley and stream of the Aksu.

3. The pass most commonly taken between the two Pamirs is, however, that which was discovered by the Russian topographer Benderski in 1883, and whose name was changed by the Russians from Andemin to Benderski in his honour. The crest is 15,130 feet. This track

mounts the Andemin confluent of the Istik, and then descends upon the Aksu valley some miles beyond the eastern end of Lake Chakmak. At the summit of the pass is a pool or lakelet of water from which—a rare occurrence—a rill flows out at either end, the one to the Great, the other to the Little Pamir. This route was followed by Littledale in 1890, and by Dunmore in 1892 ; and on their maps the pass is marked as Andemin. The crests of the Benderski and Urta Bel Passes are now the Russian frontier, as fixed by the Commission of 1895.

4. A little to the west of these passes is a fourth, the Burgutai, from which a stream, the Chelap, flows down to the western end of Lake Chakmak. This pass, however, is seldom practicable.

KIRGHIZ ON THE MARCH IN THE PAMIRS.

5. There remains a pass about which there exists great uncertainty. Gordon wrote in 1874, " A valley at the head of Lake Victoria leads to the Wurm Pass over the southern range, by which the Little Pamir, Langar, and Sarhad are reached in one and two days respectively." [1] On the other hand, in 1883, Ivanoff and Benderski " endeavoured to find the supposed pass of Varram Kotal leading to the Lake Great Pamir from Wakhan Daria (i.e. the Sarhad branch of the upper Oxus), but after several reconnaissances they were obliged to conclude that the mountains separating the Great and Little Pamir were absolutely inaccessible in this direction." [2]   Nevertheless there appears on the

---

[1] 'Roof of the World,' p. 157.
[2] Proceedings of the R.G.S., vol. vi., 1884, p. 139.

Indian Intelligence Map such a pass, named Shor Kara Jilga or Warram, which is made to debouch upon the Sarhad river between Lake Chakmak and Bozai Gumbaz, and which, I suppose, if it exists, comes down one of the many lateral gorges that I passed, and that intersect the range on that side. On the other hand, when I was marching down the right bank of the Oxus from Bozai Gumbaz, and had crossed the Dasht-i-Mirza Murad, I came to a stream which flowed into the Oxus from the north, and which was called Waram. If the maps are (as I suspect) mistaken, this may perhaps be the exit of the pass (if there is one) of the same name. I should add that later on, between 12 and 15 miles below Langar, another stream flows down a very deep *nullah* from the north into the Oxus; and that the Kirghiz in my party reported that by this *nullah* a track ran to Victoria Lake and the Great Pamir. It is possible, therefore, that there may be still unexplored passes in this part of the range. In August, 1895, some members of the British Boundary Commission party essayed to discover this or some other pass over the mountain watershed south of Lake Victoria, but met with no success, finding the range impassable in this direction, and blocked with glaciers and deep snow. In their opinion no such pass exists.

V. Passes from the Pamir-i-Wakhan to the Taghdumbash Pamir.

These I have previously described ; viz. the Wakh-jir Pass, which was crossed by Lockhart and Woodthorpe in 1885, Grombchevski in 1888, Dauvergne in 1889, Younghusband in 1891, Dunmore in 1892, and Lennard and myself in 1894, and the elevation of which is 16,100 feet; and the nameless pass in the other and more southerly fork of the Wakh-jir valley, over which Younghusband came on to the sources of the Oxus in 1891.

VI. Passes from the Little Pamir to the Taghdumbash Pamir.

1. The most familiar and easiest of these routes is that which runs from Aktash at the head of the Little Pamir, to Tashkurghan, at the head of the Taghdumbash, across another and better known Neza Tash, known also as the Shindi Pass (14,920 feet). It has been taken by many travellers.

2. A little above Aktash, a confluent on the right bank of the Aksu can be followed up, conducting to the Bayik, Beik, or Paik Pass (called by Capus Bijik-bel). It was crossed by Lord Dunmore in October, 1892, but was blocked with snow when the Frenchmen were at Aktash in April, 1887. It was explored by the members of the Boundary Commission in August, 1895 ; and falls within the frontier assigned to Russia by their agreement. The crest is 15,470 feet. The track then descends by the Bayik confluent of the Taghdumbash river on to the Pamir of that name.

3. Further to the south access can be gained from one to the other Pamir, with some difficulty and only at certain seasons of the year, by the passes at the heads of less-known nullahs which have hardly as yet been thoroughly explored. They debouch upon the Taghdumbash in the stretch between the Wakh-jir Pass and Kurghan-i-Ujad-bai. There are four of these passes—the Karachukur (taking its name from an alternative title of the Taghdumbash river), the Mukhman or Mihman-guli, the Tagharmansu (lying just outside the new frontier assigned to Russia), and the upper fork of the Kukturuk valley. They cannot, however, be considered as regular passes, and are frequently blocked by snow.

Having completed my survey of the Pamir Passes, I now return to my own journey. From Bozai Gumbaz I followed the Oxus valley down to Sarhad, a distance of 42 miles, the present outpost of Wakhan territory and Afghan rule, where the river emerges from the mountain defiles and suns itself luxuriously on the more open plain. The track, however, does not closely pursue the river gorge, whose cliffs are too steep to admit of any passage for a greater part of the way, but at a distance of 7 miles below Bozai Gumbaz bears away from the Oxus, and crosses a wide grassy upland plain known as the Dasht-i-Mirza Murad, which is marked on very early maps, and which leads down to the valley of the Waram stream.[1]   Over a second grassy upland called the

---

[1] It is at a point on the left bank of the Oxus, named Baikara, opposite to the Dasht-i-Mirza Murad, that a track runs southwards, conducting (1) to the Irshad and Chilinji Passes into Hunza; and (2) to the Khorabort Pass, leading down the Karumbar or Ishkumman valley to Gakuch, on the Gilgit river. The Irshad route is the most direct between Hunza and Wakhan, and was in frequent use both by men and ponies, until a few years ago it was blocked for animals by a change in the direction of a glacier. The pass called Irshad really consists of two passes across the same watershed, quite close to each other. One is called the Kirghiz-Uwin (16,060 feet), the other the Kik-i-Uwin (16,180 feet). The route from the Irshad comes out in the Guhjal or Upper Hunza valley, at a point between Gircha and Misgar called Khudabad.   I believe this to be the pass by which MM. Bonvalot and Capus tried to penetrate into Hunza in 1887, but their descriptions and nomenclature are so confused and inexact as to leave the matter in doubt. Anyhow, they were turned back by the snow ('Le Toit du Monde,' pp. 274, 275). The Chilinji Pass (17,000 feet), or Tash Kuprik (i.e. Stone Bridge), lies a little further to the south, and is an exceedingly difficult glacier pass, quite impracticable for animals. From Wakhan it can only be approached after the Khorabort Pass has been crossed, so that two watersheds have to be surmounted before the Upper Hunza valley is reached. After the pass has been crossed, the track joins the Irshad route. The Khorabort or Baikara Pass (15,000 feet) conducts across the main Hindu Kush watershed from Baikara to the headwaters of the Karumbar river, and thence down to Imit at the upper fork of the Karumbar or Ishkumman river. M. Dauvergne, in 1889, after crossing the Baroghil, ascended the Yarkhun river, which had been previously reported, upon native information, as rising in the same lake as the Karumbar river, and found that the Yarkhun did indeed rise in a small lake, one of the numerous Gaz Kuls, but that a low rocky watershed separated this from the larger lake, variously described as Karumbar Sar, Ishki Kul, and Zjoe Sar (?), from which issued the Karumbar stream. About the latter fact there is no doubt, although

Dasht-i-Langar we come back to the main river and to the ruins of the former settlement of Langar, a fort and two stone cairns on a hill, and some deserted dwelling-places and tombs in the valley-bottom. Below Langar the gorge becomes greatly contracted, and the Oxus, gaining volume as it descends, foams noisily along, being here unfordable. Clumps of small timber nestle in the lateral defiles. There is in one place a very bad *pari*, or cliff track, above the river, which Mr. Little-dale described in his paper. Our ponies had to be unladen and pushed and hauled up the rocks, and even so constantly slipped and fell. It is a bad place for their loads, and one of my bags was ripped clean open. Further down we again left the main gorge and diverged inland, mounting and descending successive spurs of great steepness and diffi-culty, down one of which one of our Kirghiz ponies, missing his footing, slipped and fell, and was killed instantly; until at length, mounting to the Daliz Kotal or pass (13,500 feet), we saw outspread below us the splendid vista of the Oxus valley. The river, released from its long mountain imprisonment, spread itself out in countless fibres over a wide watery plain, doubtless an old lake-bed, closed on either hand by mag-nificent snow-peaks.[1] Below us lay the terraced fields of Wakhan. Oxen,

---

the lake is said not to have a permanent existence, but to consist of an accumulation of snow-water in the spring only. But it is curious that while M. Dauvergne reported the Yarkhun river to Colonel Woodthorpe, as rising in a smaller and independent lake (*Proceedings of the R.G.S.*, vol. xii., 1890, p. 96), in his paper before the Paris Geo-graphical Society he described it as rising in a great glacier, which coincides with the information that I received from Lieutenant Cockerill, who had visited the spot (*Scottish Geographical Magazine*, 1892, p. 365). This glacier, in common with another that descends upon the Yarkhun river immediately south of the Baroghil Pass, bears the name of Chatiboi, or Chittibui, which Major Raverty ('Notes on Afghanistan,' p. 155) explains as Chitti (Hindi for "white") Bhuin (Sanskrit for "earth"), a very appropriate designation for a glacier. The rise of the Yarkhun river in this glacier is reported by some of the native travellers, whose itineraries are published by Raverty (pp. 155, 188), and is corroborated by the "Mulla," a map of whose explorations (in 1876) appeared in the *Journal of the Asiatic Society of Bengal*, 1878, part i. He depicted one branch of the river as rising in a glacier named Chatiboi, but this was the Chatiboi opposite the Baroghil. Of its more distant namesake he was not aware. Major Raverty is consequently quite mistaken, if for no other reason, in saying (p.181) that "the Dragon lake of the Chinese pilgrims Hwui Seng and Sung Yun in the Puh-hoi mountains is the *lake* of Chitti-Bui." I suspect that the Kotal or Pass of Palpi Sang, mentioned in one of Raverty's itineraries (p. 188) as "a long and narrow *darah* extending upwards for a distance of nearly ten *kuroh*, northwards from Chitti-Bui," is the Khorabort Pass, unless a confusion has arisen with the lower Chatiboi glacier, in which case it would be the Baroghil. In 1891 Colonel Yonoff, after arresting Captain Younghusband at Bozai Gumbaz, crossed the Oxus and the Khorabort Pass, which he somewhat rashly rechristened Yonoff Pass, and then, turning westwards, in the inverse direction to M. Dauvergne, descended the Yarkhun river, mounted to the crest of the Darkot Pass, and finally returned to the Pamirs by the Baroghil and Sarhad.

[1] This plain or valley was called Sarigh Chopan or Chaupan as early as the time of Baber (*vide* 'Erskine's Life,' i. 339, 340, 510), and in the chronicle of Mirza Mohammed Haidar (1543), and again by Munshi Faiz Bakhsh in 1870. The name seems now to have fallen into disuse.

goats, and sheep were being driven in at the sunset hour, and thin curls of smoke arose from the settled habitations of men.   Descending to the valley, we camped near one of the Wakhi villages in its bottom, to all of which the Afghans apply the collective title of Sarhad (10,400 feet). Their frontier post is at Chehilkund, on the right bank about 3 miles lower down, where, in a dilapidated fort on a rock, were stationed a *havildar* and a few seedy sepoys.   There is a hot sulphur spring quite close to the hamlet of Sarhad.

Sarhad was the place where, in 1890, Mr. and Mrs. Littledale, coming from the same direction as ourselves, were stopped for twelve days by the officiousness or discourtesy of the Afghan captain from

DARKOT GLACIER.

Kala Panja, 50 miles further down the river.   I had thought to have sufficiently guarded against the repetition of any such *contretemps* by having requested the Amir of Afghanistan, whose guest I was going later to be at Kabul, to send word to his officials in Wakhan of my proposed arrival.   This he had done, and the petty *havildar* at Sarhad was well aware of my identity.   Nevertheless, the opportunity of swaggering a little before the inhabitants of this remote dependency, and of humiliating the representative of a foreign nation, was too good to be lost; and the *havildar* of Chehilkund, having turned up at his leisure and offered halting apologies for a rudeness which was mani- festly designed, presently informed Lennard and myself that we were Russian spies, and that he must accordingly detain us until his commanding officer arrived from Kala Panja.   How a Russian spy

could have come by our route from Hunza, could be proposing to
re-enter British India by the Baroghil Pass, and could have been described in a letter from his own sovereign as an English traveller and
a friend of his own, the *havildar* did not attempt to explain. Leaving
him to reconcile these contradictions, and informing him of my sincere
intention to mention the matter at Kabul later on, we packed our loads,
and, having the superiority of numbers, marched off undisturbed.

I may here perhaps mention the sequel. At my first audience with
the Amir at Kabul, he raised the matter, having received my letter of
complaint, and having instituted inquiries. The reply of the now
frightened *havildar* was really so ingenious as to extort my reluctant
admiration. " He was still awaiting," he said, " the arrival of the
great English lord *sahib*, whose coming had been announced by His
Majesty the Amir, and who would no doubt appear in uniform with an
escort of 1000 men. In the mean time two of the lord *sahib's* servants
(*i.e.* Lennard and myself) had already passed through with an insignificant following. He himself would continue diligently to await the
great lord." I heard afterwards that this polite intention on the part
of the *havildar* had been frustrated by an imperative summons to
Kabul; but what may have since transpired I do not know.

Crossing the bed of the Oxus, which is here about three-quarters of
a mile in width, and fording the river, which was divided into three
main channels with from 3 to 4 feet of water, we then struck due
south into a gap in the hills, nearly half a mile wide, up which lies the
ascent to the Baroghil Pass. For nearly 3 miles the track runs through
a flat and swampy valley with abundance of grass, called Pirkhar. It
then bears a little to the west, and, gently rising, follows for 5 miles a
long and stony bay completely filled with the bed of the Pirkhar stream.
At the head of this valley two tracks bifurcate. That to the south-east
ascends to the Shawitakht or Sarkhin Pass (12,560 feet), which is an alternative to the Baroghil for travellers proceeding directly to Darkot and
Yasin, and from there descends on to the Yarkhun river, from whence a
gentle ascent of 8 miles leads to the *ailak* or summer pastures of Showar
Shur, and from thence over a glacier to the Darkot Pass (Pamir Commission, 1895, 15,200 feet; Littledale, 15,950 feet) and the route to Yasin.
The second track, which I followed, led more to the south-west, and,
after a climb of three-quarters of an hour, brought me to the rolling
saddle or dip in the main range of the Hindu Kush which is known
as the Baroghil Pass (12,460 feet). This remarkable depression is from
400 to 600 yards in width, and its crest is about 12 miles from Sarhad.
On the southern side the track descends over a gentle grassy slope,
that would provide the most admirable golf-links, to the valley of the
Yarkhun river, which it strikes some miles below the Shawitakht route.
The grassy slopes on both banks of the river are known as Dasht-i-
Baroghil. In front of one, along the entire descent, the foreground is

filled by the magnificent Chatiboi glacier, which plunges down like a prodigious frozen Niagara between two snowy peaks of the confronting range. From here, also, after fording the Yarkhun river, an ascent can be made along the edge of a great glacier to the summit of the Darkot Pass. The latter, of course, and neither the Baroghil nor the Shawi-takht, is the real defence of India on this side, since it would be almost impassable by armed men.[1]

From our camp on the Yarkhun river,[2] where Lennard and I separated, he to return to Gilgit, I to proceed to Chitral, I followed down the gorge of the Yarkhun (also called Mastuj, Chitral, Kashkar, and Kunar river) for three days, a distance of 72 miles, to Mastuj. On the first day I had to ford the river from bank to bank twelve times, and so to circumvent (I might otherwise have had to cross) six glaciers. Of these the great Chatiboi, 600 yards wide, comes right down to the edge of the river, and there towers, a precipitous wall of ice, above the foaming water.[3] Woodthorpe and Barrow, Younghusband and Cockerill were the only Englishmen who had previously descended by this route; but my journey, made at the beginning of October, proved, as the Mehtar of Chitral afterwards told me, that, though very difficult in summer, when the river is in flood and the glaciers require to be crossed, it is available from the early autumn till the late spring, and must consequently be regarded as one of the main possible routes into India. Fortunately, there is at least one place in the valley where a small body of men, taking advantage of the natural conditions, could resist a force ten times their superior in numbers. Nor is it very likely that an invading army from the north, whose objective was Chitral, would trust itself to a route that is practically confined to a single gorge for 140 miles, when the much easier and shorter route by the Dorah Pass is available. At Mastuj I joined Younghusband; and here ends that portion of my journey which I undertook in this paper to describe.

Before finally leaving the question of the Pamirs, there remains for me to redeem an earlier pledge by giving a list of the travellers of various nationalities who, from the commencement of the Christian era, are known to have visited or crossed that region. I will divide them into three classes: I. Pilgrims and travellers, Asiatic and European, down to the beginning of this century; II. English, Indian, and European explorers in the present century; III. Russian explorers in the same period.

---

[1] *Vide* the account of Littledale's difficult crossing of the Darkot in July, 1890, *Journal of the R.G.S.*, vol. xiv., 1892, pp. 24, 25. Lennard, after leaving me (in October, 1894), experienced almost equal trouble.

[2] At this point there was formerly a bridge across the river, but it was destroyed by Ali Mardan Shah, the former ruler of Wakhan, on his flight from the Afghans in 1883.

[3] This is the lower Chatiboi, the name—a familiar one for glaciers in these parts—being also sometimes applied to the neighbouring Darkot glacier. I have previously shown that it is again attached to the glacier-source of the Yarkhun river.

I. The great Central or Seric route across Asia from Bactria to China was first discovered to Europe by the expedition of Alexander the Great. The first detailed description of it was supplied by a Macedonian trader, Maes Titianus, in an account of a journey made by the factors in his employ. From this information Marinus of Tyre (A.D. 150), the predecessor of Ptolemy, determined the route which was reproduced by the latter in his great work, and which, though the identification has long been a matter of dispute, in all probability passed across the northern or central Pamirs. In the early Middle Ages, when intercommunication became more frequent, the main line of connection, which was followed by European and Asiatic embassies, and was described by Arab geographers and historians, was transferred by Turkish and Tartar ascendency to the valleys of the Jaxartes (Syr Daria) and Narin. But a few bold travellers, voyaging to and from India, kept up the knowledge of the southern or Pamir route, and at intervals through the dark ages lifted the corners of the curtain that had settled so impenetrably down upon the heart of the Asiatic continent. Among these we possess the written records of several Chinese Buddhist pilgrims, who, in their ardour for the faith which their country had adopted, undertook long and perilous journeys from China to India, to search for the sacred scriptures and commentaries of the Buddhist Canon. Their journeys have, in the revival of geographical interest which distinguished the opening of the present century, been annotated and fought over by learned scholars. But not until more recent years has it been possible to apply the test of personal knowledge and local investigation to supplement or to correct the *a priori* disquisitions of the library. These are in many cases invalidated by such an inquiry, while the credibility of the original authors, subject to inevitable deductions for Oriental exaggeration, emerges on the whole with increased credit.

The first of these pilgrims whose record has been preserved was Shih Fa-hian, a native of Wu-yang, in Shansi, who in 399 A.D. started from his native province, in company with other priests, for a quest of the Scriptures in India. Upon his return, in 415 A.D., he wrote the 'Fo-kwo-ki,' an account of his travels.[1]   Fa-hian's journey is easily

---

[1] This was first translated into French from the Chinese and edited by Abel Rémusat, with commentaries by Klaproth and Landresse, under the title 'Foue-Koue-Ki ou Relation des Royaumes Bouddhiques' (Paris, 1836). It has been translated into English from the French by Laidlay; by the Rev. S. Beal, 'Travels of Fah Hian and Sung Yun' (London, 1869); and 'Buddhist Records of the Western World' (London, 1890), vol. i. p. xi. and xxiii.-lxxxiii.; by H. A. Giles, 'Record of the Buddhistic Kingdoms' (London and Shanghai, 1877); and by J. Legge, 'A Record of Buddhistic Kingdoms' (Oxford, 1886). *Vide* also the introduction to General A. Cunningham's 'Ladak' (London, 1854); Sir H. Yule's 'Cathay and the Way Thither' (Hakluyt Society), 1866; Introduction to Wood's 'Oxus' (1872), p. xl.; a series of articles by T. Watters, in the *China Review*, 1879-80; and Major H. G. Raverty's 'Notes on Afghanistan' (1888), pp. 181, 298, 299.

traced as far as Khotan. From this point it is disputed whether its further progress to Northern India led him over or near to the Pamirs, or by a more easterly route. The following is the passage in the 'Fo-kwo-ki' : [1]—

"From Khotan they pressed onwards to the Tseu-ho country. They were twenty-five days on the road, and then they arrived at this kingdom. . . . Having stopped there for fifteen days, they went south for four days, and entered the Tsung-ling (Onion) mountains. Arriving at Yu-hwui (or Yufai), they kept their religious rest; which being over, they journeyed on twenty-five days to the Kie-sha country. . . . This country is in the middle of the Tsung-ling mountains. From there, going onwards towards North India, after being a month on the road, we managed to cross Tsung-ling. In Tsung-ling there is snow both in winter and summer. Moreover, there are poison-dragons, who, when evil-purposed, spit poison, winds, rain, snow, drifting sand, and gravel-stones. Not one of ten thousand meeting these calamities escapes. The people of that land are also called Snowy Mountain men. Having crossed Tsung-ling, we arrive at North India. On entering the borders, there is a little country called Toli. . . . Keeping along Tsung-ling, they journeyed south-west for fifteen days. The road was difficult and broken, with steep crags and precipices in the way. The mountain-side is simply a stone wall, standing up 10,000 feet. Looking down, the sight is confused, and on going forward there is no sure foothold. Below is a river called Sintu-ho. In old days men bored through the rocks to make a way, and spread out side ladders, of which there are seven hundred in all to pass. Having passed the ladders, we proceed by a hanging rope-bridge, and cross the river. The two sides are something less than 80 paces apart. Crossing the river, we come to the country of Uchang, which commences North India."

Upon the identification of the line here sketched no two writers have agreed, while several have at different times adopted contradictory explanations. Klaproth identified Tseu-ho with the Chinese Chu-ku-po of Sung Yun and the modern Kugiar, in the district of Yangi-hissar, or Yarkand. Yu-hwui he supposed to be Ladak, and Kie-sha to be Iskardu or Skardo.

Beal, in his first edition, supposed Tseu-ho to be the Yarkand river; the Yu-whui country to be the Chiltung pass (Tangetar of Benedict Göez); Kie-sha to be the Kartchou or Kie-pan-to of Hwen Thsang, and the Han-pan-to of Sung Yun (i.e. Sarikol and Tashkurghan); and he added (p. 18), "It would appear that Fah Hian crossed the Tsung-ling mountains near the Great Pamir plateau, and then, instead of keeping along the Teng-i-Badakshan of Göez, he pursued a more southerly route towards Kitaur or Chitral." Having taken his traveller to "the headwaters of the Gilgit river" (p. 68), and having identified To-li with the Ta-li-lo of Hwen Thsang, Beal then identified this with Dhir, near the river Tal (p. 18). In the same edition, on p. 70, he identified the Sinto river with the Gilgit river, and on p. 21, with the Indus—a proof of the geographical confusion into which his reasoning had led him. Wu-chang, or Uchang, he accepted as Udyana. In his

---

[1] Beal's translation in 'Buddhist Records,' vol. i. p. xxvii.-xxx.

second edition, however, Beal finds Toli to be " the valley of Darail in the Dard country," while the Sinto has now become the Swat river (p. 15).

Cunningham, on the other hand, argued strongly for an entirely different and more easterly line, taking Fa-hian over the Karakoram mountains, and identifying Kie-sha with Ladak. He then conducted the pilgrim down the Indus valley to To-li, *i.e.* Darel, and so on to India. Yule accepted this line of reasoning, and denied that Fa-hian ever entered the Oxus basin at all.

Raverty, after asserting that " Fa-hian without doubt reached the present Kashgar territory, and traversed the Karakoram Pass," declared his belief that Kie-sha was not Ladak, but the adjoining district of Balti, often called Little Tibet. To-li might, he thought, be Baltistan, Hunza, or Yasin (p. 298), though in another place he had identified the same name with the Tal or Panjkora river (p. 181). The Sinto he found to be the Gilgit river, and Uchang the Dangrak river or upper course of that stream, though elsewhere on the same page he seems to regard it as equivalent to the district of Swat. How, if Fa-hian crossed the Karakoram, he could have avoided Ladak, or how, if he came through Baltistan to Gilgit, he could have passed Hunza, or why any of these identifications should be accepted, does not appear.

I do not agree with any of the last three writers, nor, in most particulars, with the first. It is to be observed that the pilgrims travelled slowly, whichever was the route that they adopted, and that their measurements, even if correct, which may be doubted, cannot be expected to correspond (any more than do Marco Polo's) with the distances of modern itineraries; that the Tsung-ling mountains is a name applied by the Chinese to the entire mountain mass, including the Pamirs, the Hindu-Kush, and the Mustagh range, as well as the mountain belt south of them, extending from Badakshan on the west to Chinese Turkestan on the east; that Ladak, which is on the extreme eastern fringe, could scarcely be described as in " the middle of these mountains; " that Fa-hian's description of the Tsung-ling climate and conditions exactly accords with those of the Pamirs; that he employs the same name, " Snowy Mountains," as is unmistakably applied by his successor Sung Yun to the main Hindu Kush range, south of Wakhan; and, that a month after leaving Kiesha he speaks of having *crossed* Tsung-ling, which he could only have done if coming from the north, and which he would nowhere be said to have done if coming from Ladak or Baltistan. It is further to be noted that the remaining Chinese pilgrims, of whose similar journeys the records have been preserved, all travelled, on their outward or return journey, by the Pamir line; and that there is no contemporary witness to a Karakoram route. I hold, therefore, that Fa-hian did traverse some portion of the Pamir region, though what track he followed, or by what passes he crossed the main range, we have no means of ascertaining. Proceeding from the north, it is not unnatural

E

that he should strike the valley of Darel (which is probably his Toli, and the Ta-li-lo of Hwen Thsang) on the right bank of the Indus; while the latter must almost certainly be pronounced to be the Sinto of his narrative. This is the name that is elsewhere applied to the Indus by both Fa-hian and Sung Yun, and that is always given to it by Hwen Thsang, who in the 'Si-yu-ki' describes in almost identical language the same route as that taken by Fa-hian, only in the inverse direction:

" Going north-west (i.e. from Uchang) we re-ascend the Sintu river. The roads are craggy and steep; the mountains and the valleys are dark and gloomy. Sometimes we have to cross by ropes, sometimes by stretched iron chains. There are foot-bridges suspended in the air, and flying bridges across the chasms, with wooden steps let into the ground for climbing the steep embankments. Going thus 1000 li or so, we reach the river valley of Ta-li-lo." [1]

It will be seen from this passage that Uchang must lie to the east of the Indus river, an inference which is also borne out by the narrative of Sung Yun.[2] I do not see, therefore, how Uchang or Udyana can be identified, as it has been by Yule and others,[3] with Swat, which is on the western side. Swat is apparently the Suhoto of Fa-hian, and the Swat river is the Su-po-fa-su-tu of Hwen Thsang (which is the Subhavastu of the Rig Veda and the Σούαστος of Ptolemy).

There is less obscurity about the track of the next Buddhist pilgrims to India, of whose journey a record has been preserved. These were Sung Yun, a native of Tun-hwang, in Little Tibet, who was sent by the Empress of the Wei country from her capital Lo-yang (Hunan-fu) in 519 A.D., to search for sacred books in India—and his companion Hwui Sang. They returned in three years with 170 volumes of the Great Development Series, and their travels were preserved in the Chinese History of the Temples of Lo-yang.[4] Sung Yun also journeyed by way of Khotan, after leaving which he thus described his movements :

" In the 2nd year of Shan Kwai, and the 7th month, 29th day, we entered the kingdom of Chu-ku-po. . . . The limits of this country can be traversed in about five days. During the first decade of the 8th month we entered the limits of the country of Han-pan-to, and, going west six days, we ascended the Tsung-ling mountains. Advancing yet three days to the west, we arrived at the city of Kineh-you (or Kong-yu), and after three days more, to the Puh-hoi mountains. This spot is extremely cold. The snow accumulates both by winter and summer. In the midst of the mountain is a lake, in which dwells a mischievous dragon. . . . From this spot westward the road is one continuous ascent of the most precipitous character ; for 1000 li there are overhanging crags 10,000 fathoms high, towering up to the very heavens. . . . After entering the Tsung-ling mountains, step by step we crept upwards for four days, and then reached the highest part of the range.

---

[1] Beal's 'Buddhist Records,' vol. i. p. 133.

[2] Beal, Ibid., p. 102.

[3] Yule's 'Marco Polo,' vol. i. p. 173.

[4] Vide Beal's two works as before; Yule's 'Cathay,' vol. ii. p. 542; and 'Introduction to Wood's Oxus,' p. xli.; Raverty, p. 299.

From this point as a centre, looking downwards, it seems just as though one was poised in mid-air. The kingdom of Han-pan-to stretches as far as the crest of these mountains. Men say that this is the middle point of heaven and earth. . . . To the eastward of the capital of this country there is a rapid river (or a river Mang-tsiu) flowing to the north-east towards Sha-leh. The highlands of the Tsung-ling mountains do not produce trees or shrubs. At this time, the 8th month, the air is very cold, and the north wind carries along with it the drifting snow for 1000 li. At last, in the middle decade of the 9th month, we entered the kingdom of Poh-ho. The mountains here are as lofty and the gorges deep as ever. . . . The land is extremely cold—so much so, that the people occupy the caves of the mountains as dwelling-places, and the driving wind and snow often compel men and beasts to herd together. To the south of this country are the Great Snowy Mountains, which, in the morning and evening vapours, rise up like gem-spires."

There has been a general agreement among commentators, although neither the name of the Pamirs nor any possible equivalent of it is mentioned, that Sung Yun's narrative describes a march across that region. There have, however, been different identifications of the various localities named. Yule identified Chu-ku-po with Yarkand, and Han-pan-to, the Kie-pan-to of Hwen Thsang (or Khavandha, according to the restoration by Stanislas Julien), with the Chinese district bordering on the eastern Pamirs, and now known as Sarikol, whose chief town is Tashkurghan. He supposed Poh-ho to be Wakhan, but did not attempt to specify any particular passes or route, though he inclined to identify the latter with Marco Polo's track.[1] Beal followed Yule's interpretation, but identified Poh-ho with Bolor.[2] Raverty (pp. 181 and 299) said the Dragon Lake of the pilgrims was the Chatiboi lake (which, as I have before pointed out, in a footnote, is not a lake at all, but a glacier), at the source of the Yarkhun river,[3] and that the Great Snowy Mountains were the main range of the Hindu Kush, including especially Tirach-mir.

For my own part, I believe that Sung Yun approached and crossed the Pamirs from the direction of Yarkand, though by what passes he travelled it would be mere guess-work to conjecture. The Dragon Lake, which appears from his identification to be in the middle of the Pamirs, and to lie to the north and north-east of Poh-ho (Wakhan), must be one of the Pamir lakes previously described, probably Lake Victoria—an identification which is the more likely if, as I shall show, this was the lake to which Hwen Thsang, 120 years later, gave the same name. The crest of the range, to which the pilgrim climbed with so much labour, appears to be one of the Pamir dividing-ridges, which, though of

---

[1] Yule's 'Marco Polo,' vol. i. p. 184.

[2] This could hardly be, since Sung Yun speaks a little later of Po-lu-lai, which is obviously Bolor.

[3] Another argument against this identification is the statement of Sung Yun, that from the lake westward the road is a continuous and precipitous ascent. I followed it, and it is a descent the whole way.

lower elevation than some of the Hindu Kush passes, seem to have uniformly impressed all the ancient travellers with a sense of superior altitude, and of being, so to speak, the apex of the world. Sung Yun's movements, after crossing the Hindu Kush, are more difficult to trace, and I will not here pursue them.

The most famous of all these pilgrims was, however, Hwen Thsang, a native of the province of Hunan, who in 629 A.D., in the reign of Tai Tsung, the second emperor of the Tang Dynasty, set out for India, upon his own initiative, with a similar object in view. He returned successful with twenty-two horse-loads of Buddhist literature in 645 A.D., and, at the command of the Emperor, then wrote or compiled from the Sanskrit books which he had brought back with him, the ' Si-yu-ki,' or ' Records of the Western World.' This work contains a narrative of his own experiences, as well as a mass of additional information upon the countries which he either visited or heard about ; and was further supplemented by a life of the author, written by some of his pupils after his return, which corroborates and throws fresh light upon his travels.[1] With the outward journey of Hwen Thsang, which was by Tashkend, Samarkand, Balkh, and Bamian, I am not here concerned. It was on his homeward march, in the summer of 642 A.D., that, after passing through Badakshan, he came to the country of Tamositieti bordering on the Oxus, then to the country of Shang-mi, after which—

" On the north-east of the frontier of Shang-mi, skirting the mountains and crossing the valleys, advancing along a dangerous and precipitous road, after going 700 li[2] or so, we come to the valley of Po-mi-lo. It stretches 1000 li or so east and west, and 100 li or so from north to south; in the narrowest part it is not more than 10 li. It is situated among the Snowy mountains. On this account the climate is cold, and the winds blow constantly. The snow falls both in summer and spring-time. Night and day the wind rages violently. The soil is impregnated with salt, and covered with quantities of gravel and sand. The grain which is sown does not ripen; shrubs and trees are rare ; there is but a succession of deserts without any inhabitants. In the middle of the valley is a great Dragon Lake ; from east to west it is 300 li or so, from north to south 50 li. It is situated in the midst of the great Tsung-ling mountains, and in the central point of Jambudvipa.

---

[1] The European literature upon Hwen Thsang is voluminous. I may instance Abel Remusat's translation of the 'Fo-koue-ki,' with notes by Klaproth and Landresse, Paris, 1836 ; Stanislas Julien's translation of his life, 'Histoire de la Vie de H. T.,' Paris, 1853; and of the 'Si-yu-ki,' 2 vols., Paris, 1857 ; Ritter's *Erdkunde*, vol. vii., Berlin, 1837; Major W. Anderson, *Jour. of As. Soc. of Bengal*, vol. xvi., 1847; Sir A. Cunningham, ibid., vol. xvii., 1848 ; V. de St. Martin, 'Mémoire Analytique sur la Carte de l'Asie Centrale et de l'Inde,' Paris, 1858; Sir H. Yule, 'Notes on H. T.'s Account of the Principalities of Tokharistan,' 1872 ; 'Cathay and the Way Thither,' vol. i. p. 184; *Jour. R.G.S.*, vol. xlii., 1872 ; and 'Introduction to Wood's Oxus,' p. xl.; Sir H. Rawlinson, *Jour. R.G.S.*, vol. xlii., 1872 ; J. B. Paquier, 'Le Pamir' (Paris, 1876), pp. 34-45 ; Rev. J. Edkins, ' Chinese Buddhism,' London, 1880, and Rev. S. Beal, 'Life of H. T.,' London, 1888 ; and 'Si-yu-ki,' 2 vols., London, 1890.

[2] The li was a Chinese measure of distance, which varied somewhat at different times. Roughly speaking, however, we may reckon 5 li as the equivalent to one mile.

The land is very high. The water is pure and clear as a mirror; it cannot be fathomed. The colour of the lake is a dark blue, the taste of the water sweet and soft. In the water hide the *kau-ki* fish, dragons, crocodiles, tortoises. Floating on its surface are ducks, wild geese, cranes, and so on. Large eggs are found concealed in the wild desert wastes, or among the marshy shrubs, or on the sandy islets. To the west of the lake there is a large stream, which, going west, reaches so far as the eastern borders of Tamositieti, and there joins the river Fo-tsu (*i.e.* Oxus), and flows still to the west. So on this side of the lake all the streams flow westwards. On the east of the lake is a great stream which, flowing north-east, reaches to the western frontiers of the county of Kie-sha, and there joins the Si-to river and flows eastward; and so all streams on the left side of the lake flow eastward. Passing over a mountain to the south of the valley of Po-mi-lo, we find the country of Po-lo-lo. Here is found much gold and silver; the gold is red as fire. On leaving the midst of this valley and going south-east, along the route there are no men nor villages. Ascending the mountains, traversing the side and precipices, encountering nothing but ice and snow, and thus going 500 *li*, we arrive at the kingdom of Kie-pan-to." [1]

With the narrative of the traveller himself may be compared the description of his biographers, who add a few more details. According to them the Dragon Lake is 200 *li* in length, and—

" The animals that dwell in it are of infinite variety; the noise of their ten thousand cries is like the tumult of a hundred workshops. We see here birds 10 feet or so in height; eggs as large as a round water-jar, probably the same as were formerly called the *ku-koh* of the Tiu-chi. . . . This lake, moreover, is one with the Anavatapta Lake, in its north and south direction." [2]

They further add that the great river on the east actually issued from the lake (which might be inferred from Hwen Thsang).

It is clear that there are in these two narratives many exaggerations, particularly of distance and dimensions. There are also serious inaccuracies, such as the easterly outflow from Victoria Lake (supposing this to be meant) or the westerly outflow from Chakmak Lake (supposing that to be intended).[3] Nevertheless, the salient features of the account stand out as an unmistakable picture of the Pamir country, as it has already been portrayed in this paper, and leave a doubt only as to the particular valley or Pamir by which the traveller crossed it. Klaproth, Landresse, St. Julien, St. Martin, Paquier, Beal concur in identifying this with Wood's route up the main valley of the Panja to Victoria Lake. Rawlinson in his earlier writings, and Yule, prefer the more southerly

---

[1] Beal, ' Buddhist Records,' vol. ii. pp. 297, 298.

[2] Beal, ' Life of H. T.,' pp. 197, 198.

[3] Sir H. Rawlinson, in the later part of his life, wrote an essay (*Proc. R.G.S.*, 1887, p. 69), in which he argued, mainly from Mr. Ney Elias' report of his visit to Rang Kul, that the latter was the Dragon Lake of Sung Yun and Hwen Thsang. I do not think this can possibly have been the case, since Rang Kul is neither situated in the middle nor in the highest portion of the Pamirs. Above all, it has no river exit on either side, and no river anywhere near to its eastern extremity, much less flowing out of it.

track to Lake Chakmak through the Little Pamir. I entertain very little doubt of the correctness of the former hypothesis. Reasons have before been given for supposing both that Victoria Lake may once have been much larger than it now is, while in any case it is more than double the size of Lake Chakmak, and that it was also the Dragon Lake of the earlier Buddhist pilgrim Sung Yun. The stream flowing out on the west is, of course, the Pamir river, or middle confluent of the Panja. Neither the eastward-flowing drainage from the watershed beyond the eastern extremity of Victoria Lake, nor the Aksu issuing from Lake Chakmak, flow, as Hwen Thsang imagined, into the basin of the Yarkand river; but this was an error which the learned Chinaman committed in company with later and better-equipped travellers. That Victoria, and not Chakmak, Lake is alluded to is further demonstrated by the direction, viz. southeast, taken by the pilgrim, after passing the lake on his way to Kiepan-to (assuming the latter, with Yule, to be Sarikol with its capital Tashkurghan). If he had been marching by the Little Pamir route, he would have had to proceed north-east from Chakmak to Aktash. Po-lo-lo is the mysterious country so often designated Bolor.[1] By some critics its very existence, as a geographical reality, has been denied. Cunningham erroneously narrowed its identification to Baltistan or Little Tibet. I have not space here to argue the question,[2] but it can, I think, be demonstrated that Bolor, or Bilaur, was the name applied throughout the Middle Ages to the elongated belt of mountain country south of the main range of the Hindu Kush, including the valleys of Kafiristan, Upper Chitral, Yasin, Gilgit, and Hunza-Nagar (and in the pages of some writers having an even wider application). The reference to the existence of gold in this region is a further instance of accuracy. The dust is still procured by washing from the streams.

After the passage of the last of the recorded Buddhist pilgrims, there is a hiatus of six centuries in our acquaintance with Pamir topography. At the end of this time we encounter the ubiquitous footstep and the marvellously reliable pen of the great Venetian. It was in about the year 1274 A.D. that Marco Polo, his father Nicolo, and his uncle Maffeo, on their journey to the court of Kublai Khan, passed through Badakshan and then, in Marco's words—

"At the end of twelve days you come to a province of no great size, extending, indeed, no more than three days' journey in any direction, and this is called

[1] *Vide* Hwen Thsang's account of it in another part of his work. Beal's 'Buddhist Records,' vol. i. p. 135.

[2] It is discussed in Elphinstone's 'Caubul,' vol. i. p. 118; Sir H. Yule, *Jour. R.G.S.*, vol. xlii. (1872), p. 473, 'Marco Polo,' vol. i. pp. 187, 188, 'Introduction to Wood's Oxus,' p. lv.; R. B. Shaw, *Jour. R.G.S.*, vol. xlvi. (1876), p. 292; Sir A. Cunningham, 'Ancient Geography of India,' p. 84; 'Tarikh-i-Rashidi' (Ney Elias), pp. 384, 385, 405, 417; S. Beal, 'Buddhist Records,' vol. i. p. 135. But by far the most learned and authoritative dissertation is that of Raverty, 'Notes on Afghanistan,' pp. 295–308.

Vokhan.[1] . . . And when you leave this little country, and ride three days north-east, always among mountains, you get to such a height that it is said to be the highest place in the world. And when you have got to this height you find [a great lake between two mountains, and out of it[2]] a fine river running through a plain clothed with the finest pasture in the world ; in so much that a lean beast there will fatten to your heart's content in ten days. There are great numbers of all kinds of wild beasts; among others, wild sheep of great size, whose horns are good 6 palms in length. . . . The plain is called Pamier, and you ride across it for twelve days together, finding nothing but a desert, without habitations or any green thing, so that travellers are obliged to carry with them whatever they have need of. The region is so lofty and cold that you do not even see any birds flying, and I must notice also that because of this great cold, fire does not burn so brightly, nor give out so much heat as usual, nor does it cook food so effectually. Now, if we go on with our journey towards the east-north-east, we travel a good forty days, continually passing over mountains and hills, or through valleys, and crossing many rivers and tracts of wilderness, and in all this way you find neither habitation of man, nor any green thing, but must carry with you whatever you require. The country is called Bolor." [3]

Here again the main question to be determined is the identity of the lake, and as a necessary consequence of the route, indicated by the traveller. Pauthier, Rawlinson, and the majority of critics suppose the former to be Lake Victoria, and the latter the line followed in 1838 by Wood. Yule seems to have hovered between two opinions, for whereas in the text of his second edition of Marco Polo (1875) he says, " There is nothing absolutely to decide whether Marco's route from Wakhan lay by Wood's Lake or by the more southerly source of the Oxus in Pamir Kul," in his map appended thereto he marks the track along the shores of Victoria Lake ; while three years earlier he had in two in-dependent writings [4] expressed the opposite opinion, and pronounced for Lake Chakmak. Paquier alone (as far as I know) has argued in favour of a third hypothesis, viz. that Polo went by neither lake, but ascended the valley of the Shakh-dara, and somehow or other crossed the Pamirs in their centre. His argument appears to me quite unintelligible, and is in almost every point at variance with the results of recent exploration.[5]

I have at different moments been favourably inclined towards both the Victoria Lake and the Chakmak identification, and I cannot even now feel positive certainty in deciding between the two. On the whole, however, I incline to the former, or Great Pamir route. Polo evidently assumes a smaller Wakhan than the territory at present bearing that title, which begins in the bend of the Oxus at Ishkashim and ex-tends to Sarhad, a distance of about 120 miles. Seemingly, he only

[1] *i.e.* Wakhan.
[2] The words between brackets are found in Ramusio's Italian edition.
[3] Yule's ' Marco Polo,' vol. i. p. 180.
[4] *Jour. R.G.S.*, vol. xlii. (1872), p. 475, and ' Introduction to Wood's Oxus,' p. lxxiv.
[5] ' Le Pamir,' pp. 48-62.

extends it as far as Kala Panja, about half that distance. The three days' ride north-east will then be the journey up the valley of the Pamir confluent of the Panja from Langar Kisht to Victoria Lake, upon which Wood, both in coming and returning, spent four days in the dead of winter. The Venetian's lake is then Victoria Lake, and the river the Pamir river.[1] This also may be said for this hypothesis, that although the actual elevation of Lake Victoria is only some 300 feet higher than that of Lake Chakmak, yet its situation and surroundings supply a greater excuse for the illusion that it was the highest place in the world. The twelve days' ride across the Pamir can hardly be employed as an argument for one hypothesis or the other, since we have no clue as to where Polo conceived the Pamir to begin or to end. The reference to the *Ovis Poli* in the passage above quoted (from which it received its modern name) is obvious. As regards Beloro or Bolor, Marco Polo apparently protracts the area ordinarily so described to the north of the Hindu Kush, and brings it round in a great north-easterly sweep at least as far as Sarikol, if not to the borders of Kashgar territory.

Another three hundred years elapsed before we have any further record of a Trans-Pamir journey, and on this occasion, with an unconscious reciprocity that is one of the romances of history, India turned the tables upon Far Kathay, which a thousand years before had despatched its agents and pilgrims to study at Indian shrines, by herself sending out the evangelist of a newer though non-Indian faith, to reconnoitre for possible action the ground of her former conquest.

Benedict Goez, a lay Jesuit, who, though born in the Azores, had passed in the service of Portugal to India, and had there joined the mission of Jerome Xavier to the court of the great Akbar at Agra, was despatched from that place by the Provincial of his Order, with the consent of the emperor, at the begining of 1603 A.D., upon an expedition of missionary inquiry to the fabled kingdom of Cathay (Khitai). Travelling by Lahore, Peshawur, and Kabul, in the disguise of an Armenian, and in the company of a *kafila* of merchants, he crossed the Hindu Kush into Badakshan, and, passing through the Teng-i-Badakshan—one of the mountain defiles leading into the Oxus valley—came to Ciarciunar (Char Chenar?).

"From this in ten days they reached Serpanil (Sir-i-Pamir?). But this was a place utterly desolate and without a sign of human occupation; and then they came to the ascent of the steep mountain called Sacrithma.[2] None but the

---

[1] Conversely, it is possible to argue that the three days among the mountains describe the march from Sarhad to Lake Chakmak, that the river flowing from the lake is the Aksu, and that the Pamir is the Little Pamir. But in this case the error about Wakhan attains inexplicable dimensions, and the fertility of the Little Pamir seems inordinately exaggerated.

[2] I cannot suggest an identification for this name, unless it be the Sarikoram pass, by which it is conceivable that Goez, if he travelled, as I think, by the Ab-i-Panja and Little Pamir route, may have crossed from the Aksu valley on to the Taghdumbash Pamir. Yule, on the other hand, identified his route with Wood's.

stoutest of the horses could face this mountain; the rest had to pass by a round-about but easier road. . . . And so, after a journey of twenty days, they reached the province of Sarcil (Sarikol), where they formed a number of hamlets near together.[1] . . . Then in two days more they reached the foot of the mountain called Ciecialith (*i.e.* the Chichiklik Pass). It was covered deep with snow, and during the ascent many were frozen to death, and our brother himself barely escaped, for they were altogether six days in the snow here. At last they reached Tanghetar (now Tangitar), a place belonging to the kingdom of Cascar (Kashgar). . . . In fifteen days more they reached the town of Jakonich (Yakir-i-Kurghan?). . . . After five days more our Benedict reached the capital, which is called Hiarchan (Yarkand)." [2]

The above narrative, the successive stages of which cannot, I think, be mistaken, is further supplemented by some fragments of letters from Goez—who died in China—which were preserved by the Jesuit Jarric in a collection or *thesaurus* published in 1615. In one of these, dated from Yarkand, Goez spoke of the great difficulties and fatigues encountered in crossing the desert of Pamech (Pamir), the cold of which was so great that animals could scarcely breathe the air, and often died in consequence. As an antidote to this, he said that the men used to eat garlic, leeks, and dried apples, and the horses' gums were rubbed with garlic. This desert took forty days to cross—the same as Marco Polo's measurement—if the snow was extensive.

II. Nearly two and a half centuries elapsed before we meet with the next record of a journey to or across the Pamirs. This was the famous expedition of Lieut. (afterwards Captain) John Wood, of the Indian Navy, whose name fitly inaugurates the long list of British, Indian, and European explorers who, in the fifty years that have passed since his day, have familiarized us with that which was then an impenetrable mystery, not as yet irradiated by the translated records, save that of Marco Polo's journey, to which I have already, in chronological order, referred. Sent on a mission with Dr. Lord by Burnes from Kabul to Murad Ali, the Beg of Kunduz, in November, 1837, Wood proceeded from the latter place *viâ* Khanabad, Talikhan, Faizabad, Jerm, and Zebak, till at Ishkashim he touched the stream of the Oxus on February 4, 1838. Ascending the river to Kala Panja, he followed its northern confluent, the Pamir river, to its source in Victoria Lake, which he reached on February 19. His discoveries and his book reawakened public curiosity in a subject which had almost faded out of human interest, and have provided the background for the whole of our subsequent knowledge. Nor is their value in any appreciable degree impaired by the fact that the true source of the Oxus has since been found to lie elsewhere, or that Wood's scheme of the hydrography of

---

[1] Probably at or near to Tashkurghan.

[2] Yule's translation of a work by Trigault, based upon Ricci's annotation of Benedict Goez' notebook, entitled ' De Christiana Expeditione apud Sinas' (' Cathay and the Way Thither' (Hakluyt Society), vol. ii. pp. 529–562). Compare 'Introduction to Wood's Oxus,' p. xliv.; and Paquier, ' Le Pamir,' pp. 65–67.

the Pamirs was in almost every respect erroneous.[1] As the pioneer of modern exploration in these interesting regions, his name will always be held in honour. His route, as I have already argued, was in all probability identical with that which had been taken by the Chinese pilgrims Sung Yun and Hwui Sang 1300 years, by Hwen Thsang 1200 years, and by Marco Polo, 550 years, earlier.

Next upon the scene appear a number of native emissaries of the Indian Government, who, owing to the difficulty or impossibility of exploration by British officers in regions so habitually disturbed or lying so far outside the then borders of the Indian dominions, were despatched on missions of a diplomatic or scientific character in the neighbourhood of the Pamirs. Of these, the first was Abdul Mejid, a *mulla*, who was sent in 1860 with a letter and presents to Mulla Khan, ruler of Kokand.[2] Starting from Peshawur, he proceeded *viâ* Kabul and Khanabad, in Kunduz, following upon Wood's footsteps to the Oxus valley in Wakhan. At Langar Kisht he commenced the ascent of the Pamir river towards Victoria Lake, but at Jangalik (called also Yum-khana) he diverged from Wood's track, and made the first recorded passage of the Pamirs from south to north, *viâ* Khurgoshee (Khargosh Kul), Sussugh Kol (Sasik Kul), Chadur Tash (Chatir Tash), Kurra Soo (Kara Su), Moorghabee (the site of the Russian post), and Ak Baital to Kurrah Kol (Great Kara Kul), whence he proceeded by the Kizzil Arut (Kizil-art) Pass to the Alai. It was in these words that he described his crossing of the Pamirs :

"From Lungur Wakhan, fourteen weary days were occupied in crossing the steppe. The marches were long, depending on uncertain supplies of grain and water, which sometimes wholly failed. Food for man and beast had to be carried with the party, for not a trace of human habitation is to be met within these inhospitable wilds."

Of about the same date is the itinerary of a journey from Chitral and Mastuj *viâ* the Baroghil Pass, Sarhad, Langar (identical with the route which I followed in the inverse direction), Chakmak Lake, and the Little Pamir to Aktash, and thence across the Neza-tash Pass to Tash-kurghan — which was compiled by Mohammed Amin, a Yarkandi merchant, who acted as guide to the murdered Adolph Schlagintweit, and subsequently gave the itinerary to the unfortunate Hayward, who

---

[1] He wrote (p. 233): "The hills and mountains that encircle Sir-i-kol give rise to some of the principal rivers of Asia. From the ridge at its eastern end flows a branch of the Yarkand river, one of the largest streams that waters China; while from the low hills on the northern side rises the Sirr, or river of Kokan, and from the snowy chain opposite both forks of the Oxus, as well as a branch of the river Kuner, are supplied." These propositions are uniformly incorrect. The mountains encircling Victoria Lake give rise to no drainage save that of the Oxus and its main confluent the Aksu.

[2] His itinerary was published in 'Selection from the Records of the Government of India, Foreign Department, No. xxxix. Calcutta, 1863.' *Vide* also Davies' Report, Appendix xx. C.

experienced a similar fate. The report, though brief, is singularly accurate, and was published by the Indian Government in 1862.[1] A second, but more obscure itinerary, furnished by him to Pundit Manphul, a Hindu in the service of the Punjab Government, is contained in the same collection.[2] From Jangalik, on the Pamir river, it proceeds *viâ* Hamdamin and Kotal-i-Aghajan (which I cannot identify) to the valley of Tashkurghan.

It was in the same decade that the Survey Department of the Government of India began to despatch in many directions beyond the northern barriers of the Himalayas and the Hindu Kush those nameless explorers who, often under obscure generic titles, or beneath the disguise of their initials alone, have added so much to our geographical knowledge of the trans-frontier regions. One of these, known as the Mirza, started from Kabul in October, 1868, with instructions from Major T. G. Montgomerie, Deputy Superintendent of the Great Trigonometrical Survey, to penetrate to the upper Oxus, and to cross the Pamirs from west to east on his way to Kashgar.[3] Reaching the Oxus valley by way of Bamian, Khulm Tashkurghan, the Kokcha river, and Ishkashim, he ascended the river to Kala Panja, from whence, instead of diverging, as his immediate predecessors had done, up the Pamir river to Lake Victoria, he continued his exploration of the main valley of the Oxus, until he arrived, in January, 1869, at Lake Chakmak, which he designated Pamir Kul. Here all the streams were frozen, and the entire ground was under snow—a condition which led the Mirza into the mistake of supposing that the little confluent which I have described as flowing into the Ab-i-Panja at Bozai Gumbaz, actually issued from the west end of the lake. The Mirza appears also to have thought that the Aksu, instead of flowing north-west from Aktash, pierced the Neza-tash range, and flowed into the Sarikol or Tashkurghan basin, across which he himself pursued his path to Yangi Hissar to Kashgar.

The former of these errors was rectified by Ibrahim Khan, an assistant in the same government department, who, in the summer of 1870, approached the Pamirs from the opposite quarter, being sent by Forsyth from Kashmir, in anticipation of the contemplated journey of the unhappy Hayward. Proceeding *viâ* Gilgit and Yasin, he crossed the Darkot and Baroghil Passes to Sarhad; and from thence made his way, by the route which I have previously described in the inverse direction, to Langar, Bozai Gumbaz, and Lake Chakmak (which he denominated Kalsar Bam-i-Dunya), where he reported the Aksu as

---

[1] *Vide* Davies' ' Report on the Trade Routes of the North-West Frontier,' Appendix iv. B. Compare *Jour. R.G.S.*, vol. xlii., 1872, pp. 440-448.

[2] Appendix xxxi.

[3] *Vide* report of his explorations in *Jour. R.G.S.*, vol. xli. 1871, pp. 139-913. Compare Yule's ' Introduction to Wood's Oxus,' pp. xlvii., lxxiii., and 217; Paquier, pp. 113-116.

flowing out on the east, but no outlet as existing on the west.   Thence
he proceeded *viâ* Tashkurghan and Yangi Hissar to Yarkand.[1]

In the same year a more northerly track across the Pamirs was
pursued by Faiz Baksh, a native who was employed by Sir D. Forsyth
to travel *viâ* Badakshan and the Pamirs to meet him at Yarkand on the
occasion of his first mission to Yakub Beg, the Atalik Ghazi of Kashgar.
Marching from Kabul by the familiar route (Bamian, Balkh, Kunduz,
Faizabad, Zebak, Ishkashim) to the Oxus valley, he ascended *viâ* Kala
Panja and Langar Kisht to Jangalik.   Thence the stages of his journey,
as given by himself, were Dasht-i-Khar-gachi (Khargoshi?), Yolmazar,
Dasht-i-Khargoshi, Mazar-tepe, Bash Gumbaz Pass, Dasht-i-Kol Hauz
Kalan, Buztere, Istik, Aktash, Shindi, Tashkurghan.[2]   It is evident
from this description that the traveller confused two entirely distinct
itineraries.   Had he gone by the route indicated in the earlier names,
his Kol Hauz Kalan (*i.e.* Lake of the Big Pool) might have been Sasik
Kul, which, from its petty dimensions, could not conceivably have been
so called.   The later names, showing that he proceeded *viâ* Istik to
Aktash, leave it clear that he transferred to his itinerary stages which
he never actually traversed, but which lay to the north of his route,
and that in reality he proceeded by Lake Victoria (which is his Lake of
the Big Pool) and the oft-trodden route to Aktash and Tashkurghan.
This confusion does not appear hitherto to have ever attracted attention.

In the same year (1870) I have found the record of a similar journey
across the Pamirs, starting from Kabul, and proceeding *viâ* Kunduz,
Badakshan, and Wakhan to Yangi Hissar and Kashgar, of a Greek
named Dr. Potagos, whose travels were translated into French and
published fifteen years later.[3]

Next in chronological order comes the first really scientific expedition to the Pamirs undertaken by British agents, viz. the journeys of
Captain (now Colonel) Trotter, Lieut. (now Sir Thomas) Gordon, Captain
(now Colonel) J. Biddulph, and Dr. Stolicza, who were detached from
Sir D. Forsyth's second mission to Kashgar in 1874, to make a detailed
exploration of what was still at that time universally designated the
Pamir Plateau.   The records, in the shape of reports, books, and papers,
that were left by the various members of this expedition have been
cited in the opening portion of this essay, and constituted the first
serious British contribution to the scientific knowledge of the entire
region.   Marching *viâ* Sarikol and Tashkurghan, they reached Lake
Chakmak on April 5, 1874, finally setting at rest the disputed questions
as to the river outlet or outlets from that lake.   Thence Gordon, Trotter,

---

[1] *Proc. of the R.G.S.*, vol. xv., 1870–71, p. 387.

[2] *Jour. R.G.S.*, vol. xlii., 1872, pp. 464–466; Yule's 'Introduction to Wood's Oxus,'
p. l.

[3] Dr. Potagos, 'Dix Années de voyages dans l'Asie Centrale,' etc.   Traduction:
Paris, 1885.

and Stolicza went north to Lake Victoria and the Istik river, while Biddulph marched southwards by Sarhad to examine the Baroghil Pass, and ultimately returned *viâ* Lake Chakmak to rejoin his companions. Meanwhile Trotter had despatched Abdul Subhan, a native assistant surveyor, to investigate the course of the Oxus through Shighnan and Roshan; to whose report upon the respective volumes of the Panja and the Bartang (Murghab) at Kala Wamar I have previously referred.

A different route was taken, at the expense of a fresh geographical error, by a native *employé* of the Indian Survey Department, in 1880. This was one M. S., a Pir, who ascended the Bartang valley from Kala Wamar, in September of that year, as far as Sarez, where, from some inexplicable error, he reported that the source of that river lay, thereby throwing once again into confusion the as then unsolved question of the three-in-one Aksu-Murghab-Bartang.[1]

In 1885, Mr. Ney Elias, already famous for his Asiatic travels, was despatched by the Indian Government upon a special mission to Chinese Turkistan, included in his orders being an instruction to explore and report upon the Afghan districts of the upper Oxus. With characteristic intrepidity, he sketched out for himself and followed an entirely original track from east to west across the Pamirs, with the results of which the public has only been made familiar by hearsay. Starting from Kashgar in September, 1885, he proceeded by Little Kara Kul and Rang Kul (being the first Englishman to visit those lakes) to the Alichur river and Yeshil Kul, whence he descended the Ghund valley to Kala Bar Panja, on the Oxus. Following that river northwards to Kala Wamar and the boundaries of Darwaz, he then struck eastwards up the Bartang basin to the base of the Kudara valley. Returning thence, he ascended the left bank of the Oxus to Ishkashim, whence, *viâ* Zebak and Badakshan, he proceeded westwards through Afghan Turkestan to join the Anglo-Russian Boundary Commissioners, whom he encountered near Herat, in January, 1886. His journey, though inaccessible in its published form to the public, added greatly to the geographical and political knowledge in possession of the Indian Government, and has contributed substantial additions to all subsequent maps.

In the following year, *i.e.* 1886, Colonel (now Sir W.) Lockhart, Colonel Woodthorpe, Captain Barrow, and Dr. Giles, who had occupied the year 1885 in their interesting mission to the court of Aman-ul-Mulk, Mehtar of Chitral, and had explored the southern slopes and valleys of the Hindu Kush, returned to the same destination by a circuitous march from Gilgit (for the most part over the track which I followed and have described) *viâ* Hunza-Nagar, the Kilik, the Wakh-jir Pass, the Oxus valley, Kala Panja, and Wakhan. Theirs was the first scientific report of the main course of that river from its glacier source (which, however,

---

[1] Report of the Indian Survey Department, 1881–82.

they did not visit, but which was mapped by a native surveyor) to the great bend at Ishkashim. It is enshrined in a monumental government publication.

In the spring of 1887, the three French travellers, MM. Bonvalot, Capus, and Pepin, already well known for their travels and writings in other but less remote parts of Central Asia, made the first recorded passage of the Pamirs from north to south, *i.e.* from Russian territory in Ferghana, to British Indian territory in Chitral. Descending into the Alai valley by the Taldik Pass, they crossed the Kizil-art on to the Great Kara Kul, whence by the Uzbel Pass they proceeded to Rang Kul, and by the Kara-su and Aksu valleys to Aktash, Lake Chakmak, and the Little Pamir. Continuing to Bozai Gumbaz and Sarhad, after an unsuccessful attempt upon the Irshad Pass, they crossed the Baroghil and descended the Yarkhun river to Mastuj, whence they were rescued in an almost destitute condition by the kindly offices of Lord Dufferin, at that time Viceroy of India, and safely escorted to Simla. Their books, which do not err on the side of generosity, have been already alluded to.

From this time onward, attracted by the increasing notoriety, or impelled by the political fascination, of the region, the stream of English explorers in the Pamirs swell rapidly. In the summer of 1888, St. George Littledale, a subsequent Gold Medallist of this Society, paid his first visit to the Pamirs, in pursuit of *Ovis Poli*, penetrating, under Russian patronage, from the north as far as the Great Kara Kul. In 1889 he undertook, with Mrs. Littledale (the first, and so far the last, English lady who ever saw the Pamirs), a more adventurous journey, crossing the region from north to south, and passing *viâ* Kara Kul, Victoria Lake, Lake Chakmak, Sarhad, the Baroghil and Darkot Passes to Kashmir. At Kara Kul, in 1888, he encountered Messrs. O'Connor, H. Ridgway (Americans), and H. Dauvergne (a French merchant, long resident in Kashmir), who, entering from the same quarter, were making a tour of the Central Pamirs. In 1889, in the same neighbourhood he met Major Cumberland, who had separated from Captain Bower and H. Dauvergne on the Taghdumbash Pamir, at the same time that Dauvergne had started on his return to Gilgit by the Wakhjir Pass, the sources of the Oxus, the Baroghil, the sources of the Yarkhun and Karumbar rivers, and the Ishkumman gorge. In the same year, *i.e.* 1889, two other Frenchmen, Visconte de Breteuil and L. Richard, were engaged on a sporting expedition with H. Ridgway on the southern Pamirs.

It was at about the same time that Captain F. E. Younghusband, like Bower, a Gold Medallist of the Society, commenced those explorations of a semi-political, semi-geographical character in the Pamir region which extended over three years, and were diversified by the opposite features at one time of the peaceful reading of a paper before the Royal Geographical Society, at another of his own forcible arrest and expulsion from Bozai Gumbaz by Colonel Yonoff and his predatory band. This was on August 17, 1891, Lieut. Davison (since dead) being simultaneously arrested and deported from the Alichur Pamir, whither he had been despatched on a reconnoitring mission by Younghusband. In 1890 the latter had traversed the central Pamirs with Mr. G. Macartney, the British representative at Kashgar; in 1889 he had broken ground on the Taghdumbash.

I now pass to more recent visitors, the majority of whom have been attracted to the Pamirs by the love of sport, or, in other words, the pursuit of *Ovis Poli*, though to these preoccupations some of their number have added the quest of geographical or scientific knowledge. In 1891 H. Lennard and R. Beech, and separately from them Lieut. J. M. Stewart, were on the southern Pamirs. In 1892 Lord Dunmore and Major Roche, as described in the former's book, crossed the Pamirs from south-east to north-east, entering from Yarkand and emerging at Kashgar. In 1893 a Frenchman, Baron de Ponçins, marched from north to south, and came down into India. In 1894, which was the year of the journey undertaken by Lennard and myself, which I have here described, Comte de Bylandt, a Dutchman, also crossed from north to south. In 1894-5 Dr. Sven Hedin, the well-known Swedish traveller and scientist, from the base of Pamirski Poste, or the Russian fort at Murghabi, conducted these explorations of Mustagh Ata to which reference has before been made. Other sportsmen, coming from Yarkand and Tashkurghan, have shot *Ovis Poli* on the Taghdumbash Pamir, but, having penetrated no further into the true Pamir country, cannot be counted here. Finally, in the summer and early autumn of 1895, Major-General Gerard, Colonel Holdich (in command of the survey party), Major Wahab, Dr. Alcock, and Captain McSwiney, representing Great Britain on the Pamir Boundary Commission, which was appointed to demarcate the frontier between Lake Victoria and the Chinese border above the Taghdumbash, completed our scientific knowledge, and rectified the cartography of the southern Pamirs, in conjunction with Major-General P. Shveikovski, the chief Russian representative, M. Ponafidin, Colonel Galkin, Colonel Zaleski, and M. Benderski, of earlier topographical fame. Their report is, I believe, likely to be published as a Parliamentary paper. These are, so far as I know, the only English and European (other than Russian) travellers who have been either tempted by pleasure or impelled by duty to a peregrination of the inhospitable " Roof of the World."

III. Finally, I turn to the Russian explorers, who, though appearing on the field much later than their British or Anglo-Indian rivals, have yet during the last twenty years, owing to the superior proximity of their base, and to the consistent patronage of the Imperial Government, made a more thorough and detailed survey of the northern and central Pamirs, with occasional rushes and excursions to the southern

or more British zone, than British officers have ever been able to do
of the regions lying beyond the recognized frontier of Hindostan. In
the majority of places the Russians have not been the first in point of
time to arrive; but, having arrived, they have commonly effected more.

It was as the sequel to her rapid and all but unresisted conquest of
the Central Asian Khanates in the decade following 1860, that the
pioneers of Russia, pushing their way eastwards through the province of
Ferghana, first struck the Pamir region from the north. Fedchenko, in
1871, made his way to the Alai valley, but did not cross the Trans-Alai
mountains, though he named their highest peak, in honour of the Russian
Commander-in-chief, Mount Kaufmann. He did not, however, touch
the Pamirs proper, which were reserved for his successors.

In 1876 the famous Skobeleff was placed by Kaufmann in command
of the Alai expeditionary force, with instructions to explore and plant
the Russian flag in these little-known outskirts of the new Russian
dominion. The party consisted of Captain Kostenko as geographer and
statistician, A. Bonsdorf as geodesist, W. Oshanin for natural history,
Colonel Lebedeff of the Corps of Topographers, and others. Starting
from Gulcha, the then Russian outpost, in August, 1876, the main body
of the force, under Skobeleff, did not proceed beyond the Alai valley, but
from their camp there Prince Witgenstein, having been sent on with
a flying column across the Trans-Alai, was the first European in modern
times to see the Great Kara Kul, which he reached on August 12.
Thither he was speedily followed by Kostenko, who then started for
Rang Kul, but, owing to lack of provisions, did not get beyond the Uzbel
Pass, from the summit of which he saw the great peak of Mustagh Ata
on August 19. Meanwhile Witgenstein, marching due south from Kara
Kul, had proceeded as far as the Tuyuk or Ak Baital Pass. This was
the limit of Russian exploration in that year.

In the following year the first really qualified scientific expedition
was despatched by General Kaufmann, its operations extending into two
years. The control of the party was given to N. Severtsoff, with particular charge of physical geography and zoology; Schwarz undertook
the astronomical and magnetic observations; Skassy was topographer;
Colonel Kushakevich was botanist and entomologist; and Captain
Skorniakoff was in command of the escort. Leaving Tashkend in September, and Osh in October, 1877, they crossed the Alai by the Shart-
dawan, and the Trans-Alai by the Kizil-art, and explored the region
between the mountains and Kara Kul. In 1878 they reassembled near
that lake, being joined there by Rudonef, and then marched south by
the Tuyuk Pass to Rang Kul, whence they descried the two great
mountain masses towering up to the east beyond Little Kara Kul, the
northernmost of which had been roughly fixed by Hayward on his road
from Yangi Hissar to Kashgar in 1868, and by Trotter from the same
neighbourhood in 1874; while the southerly peak had been seen by

Kostenko from the Uzbel in 1876, and by Trotter and Gordon from Tashkurghan in 1874. The second of these, as has before been pointed out, is the true Mustagh Ata. From Rang Kul the party turned south-westwards, and explored the Sarez and Alichur Pamirs, visited Yeshil Kul, discovered the small cluster of lakes at its eastern extremity, and for the first time connected the Russian with the British surveys, four years earlier, of Trotter. Scarcity of provisions again compelled an early return, and in September the expedition was back at Gulcha. Severtsoff gave it as his opinion that in the inner Pamirs the elevation, which he computed to have risen 600 feet in the last 12000 years, is still going on.[1]

Meanwhile, in 1878 two other Russian expeditions had, from different quarters, assailed the same objective. Crossing the Trans-Alai range by the Ters-agar Pass, to the west of Mount Kaufmann, J. Mushketoff descended upon the valley of the Muk-su, or southern confluent of the Kizil-su, but was prevented from penetrating further southward by the rebellion that had broken out in Shighnan and Darwaz after the death of the Atalik Ghazi, Yakub Beg. Turning eastwards, he visited Kara Kul, and returned from thence to the Alai. His geological observations showed the northern part of the Pamir region to consist of granite, metamorphic clay, and mica slate, overlaid with strata of the trias formations, the direction of the granite upheavals being north-east.

In the same summer another party, consisting of Oshanin, Nevelski (botanist), and Rodionoff (surveyor), projected a crossing of the entire Pamirs from north-west to south *viâ* Poliz and the Sel-sai; but were stopped by difficulties and accidents, and compelled to return in September to Altyn Mazar, having only surveyed what may be called the northern boundary of the region.

When, in 1878, General Abramoff was placed in command of the military expedition which was despatched by Kaufmann in that year, simultaneously with the Kabul mission, to execute an anti-English diversion in the Pamirs, Matvaieff, the military topographer attached to the party, is said to have surveyed the western confines of the Pamirs, and to have crossed the Oxus into Badakshan. Whether he penetrated the Pamirs strictly so called, I have been unable to ascertain. The names of Dr. Regel, botanist, and Kossiakoff, military topographer, who in 1881 entered Darwaz from Karategin, and in 1882 wintered in Shighnan, should not be altogether omitted in this context, although their labours were directed rather to the Pamir borderlands than to the Pamir itself.

We next come to the second great official Russian expedition, which was commissioned in 1883 to complete the labours of Severtsoff and his

---

[1] Vide *Isvestia Imp. Russ. Geogr. Obsh.* (St. Petersburg), 1879; *Zapiski* of Ditto, vol. xiii., 1886, and vol. xv., 1887; and Severtsoff's posthumous work, in Russian entitled 'Orographical Sketch of the Pamir Mountain System.'

earlier band of pioneers. Its members were Captain Putiata of the general staff, Ivanoff as geologist, and Benderski as topographer. Leaving Tashkend in May, and Osh in June, 1883, they marched to Kara Kul, whence Putiata and Benderski proceeded *viá* Bulun Kul, Little Kara Kul, and the Tagharma valley to Tashkurghan, and from there by the Neza-tash Pass down the Aksu to Ak-baital; while Ivanoff's route lay *viá* Rang Kul, Little Kara Kul (whence he examined Mustagh Ata), and the Aksu to the same destination. Again separating, Putiata went *viá* Buz-tere to the Alichur, and Yeshil Kul, and then made a circuit by the Koh-i-tezek Pass and the Togaz-bulak confluent of the Ghund. Ivanoff and Benderski ascended the Kara-su, crossed the second Neza-tash, ascended the Chish-tiube confluent of the Istik, and came down upon Lake Chakmak and the Little Pamir, whence they mounted the Ab-i-Wakhan for a short distance, returning *viá* the Urta Bel to Lake Victoria, and by the Bash-gumbaz to Alichur. Here the parties reunited, and returned by the Khargosh Pass to the Great Pamir, and down the Pamir river to Yol-mazar. From this point Putiata and Benderski retraced their footsteps and discovered the Andemin or Benderski Pass between the Great and Little Pamirs. Ivanoff ascended the Mas river, re-examined the Yeshil Kul basin, and marched down the Ghund river as far as Sardim, the highest inhabited village of Shighnan. Having completed their surveys of the central and southern Pamirs, the expedition contemplated a southerly excursion to the Baroghil and Chitral; but finding this impossible owing to the forward movement of the Afghan forces into Shighnan, they ascended the Kudara river, examined the great Fedchenko glacier, and returned to Russian territory in December of the same year, having contributed to Pamir cartography more accurate and detailed information than any preceding or subsequent expedition.[1]

In 1887, the brothers Grum-Grjimailo, naturalists, traversed the northern Pamir from west to east, visiting the Kudara river and Rang Kul, whence they crossed to Tashkurghan, and explored the upper waters of the Yarkand Daria.

Five years later Captain Grombchevski, a Polish officer in the Imperial Guards, who had been adjutant to Skobeleff in 1876, and later had officiated as assistant-governor at Marghilan, and frontier commissioner in Ferghana, commenced the series of Pamir and trans-Pamir explorations which for a time rendered his name so familiar to the British public. In 1888 he crossed the Hindu Kush, as previously mentioned, by the Kilik Pass, and penetrated to Hunza, where he endeavoured to win over Safdar Ali Khan, then Raja, to the Russian alliance. In 1889 he entered by Karategin and Darwaz as far as the frontiers of Shighnan, where the Afghan incursion put a stop to his

---

[1] *Invest. Imp. Russ. Geog. Obsh.*, 1884.

plans of further advance. Proceeding eastwards by the Alichur, Great, and Little Pamirs, he crossed the Bayik Pass on to the Taghdumbash, and while on the Raskam Daria encountered Younghusband, on his march from the Shimshal Pass to the Taghdumbash. When he reached Shahidulla, Grombchevski, finding the winter coming on, demanded permission for himself and his armed escort to descend into Kashmir, and was very much offended when this permission was refused by the British Resident. In 1890 Grombchevski and Younghusband again met in Yarkand. In 1892 he was appointed Governor of Osh, and has probably spent more years in and about the Pamirs than any living man.

In 1889 Prince Galitzin passed as a private traveller across the Pamirs on his way to British India. In 1891 Colonel Yonoff commenced the series of military parades in the Pamir region which were intended to impress the few inhabitants and the surrounding peoples with the might of Russian arms, and which resulted in the permanent occupation by the Russians of the Murghabi fort, or Pamerski Poste, so frequently already mentioned. Finally, in 1895 the Boundary Commission, under General Shveikovski, already cited, completed the arrangements under which, by agreement between Great Britain and Russia, the bulk of the Pamirs have passed into the final possession of the latter power, the Little Pamir remaining as a sort of unpeopled buffer-state between. The era of exploration and discovery in this celebrated region may therefore now be said to have come to an end. The boundaries having been determined, there survives no legitimate cause of political quarrel; and the mystery and romance of the fabled Roof of the World having been extinguished by the theodolite and the compass, and superseded by the accurate delineation of scientific maps, few persons will probably in future aspire to visit a region where fresh laurels are scarcely to be won, and where the necessities of even a traveller's existence are so scant. On the threshold of this new epoch, I hope that some advantage may be served by the attempt which I have made in these pages to resume, expound, and collate the references of the past in the light of modern knowledge, and to show what the Pamirs really are, as viewed from the double standpoint of historical mention and personal experience. I shall never again visit that distant country myself, but I shall be grateful if the studies of ten years have assisted to simplify any of its features or its problems to the understanding of others. The map which accompanies this paper marks, I would fain believe, a great advance on any previously accessible publication, either in Russia or England, containing, as it does, a mass of information only to be found in Government bureaux, and never previously made public.

PRINTED BY WILLIAM CLOWES AND SONS, LIMITED, LONDON AND BECCLES.